# A PRACTICAL GUIDE TO

# PATIOS
## AND THEIR
# SURROUNDS

# A PRACTICAL GUIDE TO

# PATIOS
## AND THEIR
# SURROUNDS

Bramley Books

# Introduction

The increased use of attractive containers means that it is possible to form a garden almost anywhere, whether on a balcony, a small patio or even on a window-ledge. A diverse range of plants are suitable for growing in containers. Strawberries, tomatoes and some roses, for example, are among the plants that can be successfully grown in hanging baskets.

There are many types of container to choose from. Large, wooden tubs have, for many years, offered homes for shrubs and small trees, while clay pots are frequently planted with tender plants. Window boxes are also a popular way to brighten the outside of houses. In the past they were often planted with sweet-smelling plants like mignonette to combat other, less pleasant, smells. Although it is no longer necessary to grow fragrant plants in containers close to the house for this reason, the tradition for doing so has remained.

Less conventional containers can also be used to grow plants in and can look spectacular. Old stone sinks, for example, can be used to great effect on patios, where they can be planted with miniature conifers, bulbs and alpine plants. When using containers like this, however, it is important to use a well-drained compost covered with a thin layer of gravel chippings to prevent rain splashing on the soil on the surface. Miniature water gardens can also be created in large, wooden tubs or stone sinks, but care is needed in the selection of water plants.

Giving sound practical advice on how to create an attractive patio and filled with useful tips for making the most of the surrounding area, this book gives a good introduction to the techniques of container gardening.

© Marshall Cavendish 1995

Some of this material has previously appeared in the Marshall Cavendish partwork **My Garden**.

4385
This edition published 1996 by Bramley Books
All rights reserved
Printed in Singapore
ISBN 1-85833-543-4

# Contents

# Creating Hanging Baskets

**Create a lovely visual effect with a beautiful basket that can be hung wherever you need a splash of summer colour.**

Eric Crichton

John Glover

Jerry Harpur/EWA

Hanging baskets can be used to brighten up a bare wall, giving a view of flowers and foliage from windows that would otherwise face only bricks. They can make a 'garden' on the side of a house or dreary back yard where there is no room to grow any plants at ground level.

Hanging baskets can be suspended from a pergola to give a floral walkway down a garden path or across a patio. They are especially good in this instance, to add summer colour when the climbers grown on the pergola flower early or late in the season and have little to offer except foliage in high summer.

## What sort of basket?

Traditionally, hanging baskets were made from galvanized wire and would be lined with sphagnum moss. Nowadays black polythene is often used instead of, or together with, the moss. The major advantage in using moss is that it is more attractive than black plastic.

A third alternative is to buy ready-made moulded liners of compressed peat and fibre which can be placed straight into your basket.

The basket itself is usually made from plastic or wire and can either be meshed or solid. The main advantage of mesh baskets, is, of course, that plants can be inserted through the gaps, making a spectacular display. Solid baskets,

*Basketworks: enliven a wall clad with green leafy climbers (above) by adding a softly coloured basket arrangement; use a riot of red against pale brickwork (above left); a porch is the perfect place to hang a showpiece basket (left).*

Tim Woodcock

## PLANTS FOR BASKETS

For the best effect, plant trailers such as ivies around the edge, and slightly taller plants in the centre. Here are some examples of suitable plants:

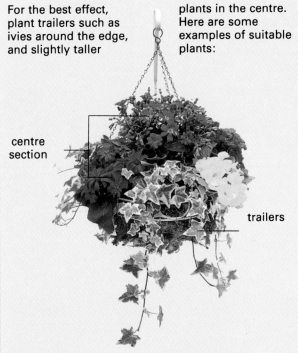

centre section

trailers

### CENTRE SECTION

calendula (marigold)
fuchsia (non trailers)
petunia
French marigold
tobacco plant
pansy
begonia
geranium
cineraria
lobelia (non trailers)
dwarf snapdragon
busy Lizzie
coleus
calceolaria

### TRAILERS

lobelia (trailing varieties)
small-leaved ivies (variegated and non-variegated)
*Helichrysum petiolatum* (semi-trailer)
ivy-leaved geranium
nasturtium
fuchsia (trailing)
dwarf sweet peas
*Verbena tenera*
petunia
mimulus
*Campanula fragilis*

though slightly easier to plant, are often not quite so effective. The solid plastic versions are like large flower pots and usually have rigid plastic wires and a drip saucer attached to the bottom. Others are made from fibre and resemble heavy-duty versions of the peat and fibre liners. These will only last for a couple of seasons, but are inexpensive, look natural and are extremely easy to use.

### Making an impact
A wide selection of both flowering and foliage plants make much more of an impact than just two or three plants of different varieties.

Conversely, try just one kind of plant in a single colour for a really striking effect. Some of the best plants for this are petunias or fibrous-rooted begonias for a sunny position and busy Lizzies or fuchsias for a shady site.

Plan your baskets with your window boxes or other containers in mind; either match them in colour and texture for a harmonious effect or contrast them completely for an equally attractive and very arresting design. Try matching your baskets to complement their surroundings, picking up

## WATERING TIPS

● Put a few lumps of charcoal into the moss base of your basket to keep water fresh.

● Fit an adjustable spray to the end of the hose for fine watering.

● A bamboo cane tied in several places along the end of a hosepipe will keep the pipe rigid, making watering a high container much easier.

# LONG-LASTING

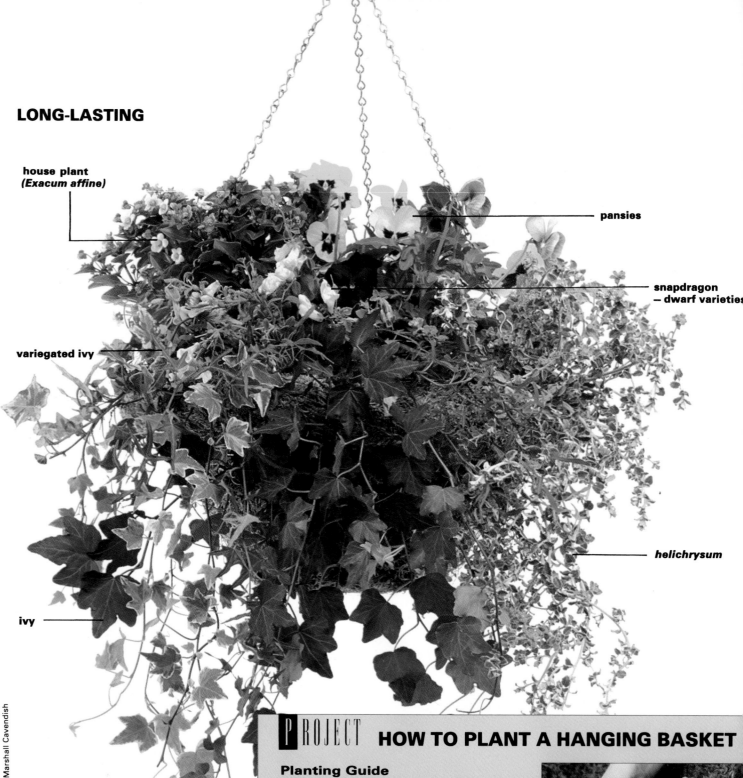

house plant
(*Exacum affine*)

pansies

snapdragon
— dwarf varieties

variegated ivy

helichrysum

ivy

## Long-lasting Basket

To fill a basket 25-30cm/10-12in in diameter, you will need approximately four pansies, six ivies (some plain, some variegated), one or two dwarf antirrhinums and three helichrysums.

Choose reasonably mature plants so that you will not have to wait too long for the basket to 'bush out'.

While you are waiting for plants to spread, fill any gaps with small, potted plants that can easily be removed. This *Exacum affine* is really pretty, but tender, so place in an outdoor arrangement only in very mild or sheltered conditions.

This basket will look good all summer long and last well into autumn, until the first frosts.

## ℙROJECT  HOW TO PLANT A HANGING BASKET

### Planting Guide

Stand the basket on an upturned pot to help steady it as you work.

The sphagnum moss should be damp; position it with the greenest parts facing outwards.

Before adding special potting compost, you may like to place an old saucer or a circle cut from a plastic bag in the base of the basket as a further aid to moisture retention and a few lumps of charcoal, which helps to prevent water becoming stagnant.

Firm the roots of plants into the compost as you work. When you have finished planting, stand the basket in a large bowl or container of water until it is thoroughly soaked. Soak once a week thereafter, and water daily using a can with a fine rose.

EWA

**1** *Place basket on a plant pot and line with damp sphagnum moss. Push trailers through sides.*

# BOLD AND BRIGHT

geranium

busy Lizzie

begonia — fibrous rooted

ivy

Verbena tenera

Cut a circle of plastic for the base of the basket to aid moisture retention. Arrange outer rim plants and firm in.

**3** Position the central plant, which should stand taller than those surrounding it. Firm in, water the basket and allow to settle and drain before hanging in your chosen location.

## Bold and Bright Basket

This basket displays bold and pastel coloured plants in greens and pinks. The two-colour theme makes just as great an impact as baskets with a mass of colours. This selection of plants fills a 25cm/10in basket with a beautiful array of foliage and leaves.

You will need three or four busy Lizzies and the same number of begonias, two small geraniums, about six verbenas and three or four ivies.

Arrange the plants on the surface of this basket before putting in their final positions to show off a balanced display.

Plant the verbenas first, ensuring that they are evenly spaced around the basket, their trailing stems poking through the sides. Follow these with the different ivies.

Finish your basket by planting the busy Lizzies, begonias and geraniums which will form a bushy mass of flowers and foliage on top.

on the colour of your garden pots for example.

A basket filled with moist compost and well-developed plants weighs a considerable amount. It must be hung from a very strong support, on chains, from a bracket screwed either to a wall or to the sides of a doorway, or hung from the underside of a porch, balcony, arch or pergola. You will need to use a drill with a masonry bit to plug the wall before screwing anything to it.

### Watering ways

Compost in hanging baskets dries out rapidly in hot weather and needs watering once or even twice a day. An effective way of doing this is to take down the basket and stand it in a bowl of water for 15 minutes or so until the compost is thoroughly damp. This will quickly revive a flagging display. You should not do this, however, if the basket is too heavy or it contains trailing plants which could easily be crushed in the process.

There are special devices available which allow baskets to be lowered on a pulley for

*A basket (right) full of lobelia and busy Lizzie in brilliant shades of pink with just a few touches of white makes a most attractive, colour-coordinated display.*

Tim Woodcock

*Make the most of the smallest of garden spaces with lots of flowering baskets. Creating a theme makes a bold statement, such as here, where trailing basket geraniums (below) link prettily with the tub geraniums beneath.*

easy access. Alternatively, a pump can with a two litre bottle and long tube makes watering easy without lowering, and so does a watering lance fitted on to the end of a garden hose – or try an old washing-up liquid bottle as a cheap option.

Even after heavy bursts of rain baskets may need watering as plant growth may have prevented rain reaching the roots, or house eaves may have kept the rain off all together.

### Keep them sweet

When you water your basket, take the opportunity to cut off

EWA

10

*This simple but effective planting scheme (left) uses foliage as much as flowers for its impact. Soft pink trailing geraniums and silvery helichrysums show up particularly well against a dark brick wall.*

EWA

*A newly erected fence can look a bit stark while you're waiting for plants to grow up against it. Just the place to have a hanging basket (left), or even two or three.*

Tim Woodcock

the dead heads from flowering plants and, as the season progresses, pinch back any very vigorous plants, such as *Helichrysum petiolatum* or nasturtiums, as they can smother their neighbours if left to grow unchecked.

You may need to remove plants that have died or finished flowering. Rather than leave gaps in the basket, ease some small plants such as fibrous-rooted begonias or violas into the spaces left behind.

### Little pests!

Keep a watch out for weeds and remove them at once. You can deter birds from pulling out young plants by pushing a number of short twigs into the compost, then winding black thread, lattice-fashion, around them to create 'netting'.

Aphids (green or black fly) are the most common pests you are likely to encounter. They must be dealt with quickly otherwise they will soon multiply. To avoid using insecticide, spray the aphids forcefully with soapy water and repeat the treatment as necessary.

### Bloomin' beautiful

Colour scheming does not have to be confined to the house. Just as you match the colours of carpets, curtains and cushions, let your imagination flow and indulge your creativity by planting baskets which reflect the colours of your garden. Most small plants which will flourish in a container will grow happily in a hanging basket – so use them to the full.

For something really different try growing fruit or vegetables in a basket. Use dwarf or mini tomatoes, or Sweetheart strawberries to make a vibrant display of red and green. Make a herb basket and hang it by the kitchen door so that your fresh supply is near at hand. Fill it with parsley, a mix of silver, gold and green thymes, purple and gold sages and other colourful herbs. Add bright nasturtiums and remember the leaves, flowers and seeds are edible.

Hanging baskets need not be banished in autumn and winter. If kept in a sheltered spot, replace summer displays with small leaved variegated ivies or euonymus. Plant early bulbs like crocuses and snowdrops to welcome the spring and replace these later with coloured primroses, pansies, pot-grown hyacinths or dwarf daffodils – to take you into summer.

Stylish hanging baskets can be created using only one species of plant. Diascia (above), characterised by its distinctive tubular-shaped flowers, and the brightly coloured Mimulus 'Malibu' (left) have been planted to maximum effect in hanging baskets, giving stunning displays.

# Unusual Hanging Baskets

**Experiment with unusual plants and new ways of displaying them, to create stunning hanging baskets with individual character, flair and style.**

Photos Horticultural

Hanging baskets have been popular for many years. But few people like to repeat an old display, however successful it was. Now, manufacturers are coming out with novel styles of baskets, and seed firms offer a tremendous range of unusual trailing plants, short climbers and other plants seen at their best in baskets. So, with a little experience of basic 'hanging gardens' under your belt, why not branch out and try something more distinctive?

Experiment with different plants, innovative planting schemes, and new kinds of basket to create something stylish that will not only stamp the garden with your personal flair, but impress visitors and keep the neighbours guessing!

## Multi-storey baskets

Instead of the single large baskets you often see, why not group several smaller baskets

*Rather than planting the traditional single hanging basket, create a cluster of baskets (above) at different levels. Pack them full of flowers of contrasting colours and shapes for a stunning display that is guaranteed to revitalize any garden in need of a face-lift.*

# UNUSUAL BASKET PLANTS

## Climbers
Black-eyed Susan (*Thunbergia alata*) – bright orange-yellow, single flowers **HHA**
Canary creeper (*Tropaeolum peregrinum* syn. *T. canariense*) – yellow frilly flowers **HA**
Morning glory (*Ipomoea*) – huge circular flowers, various colours **HHA**
Purple bell vine (*Rhodochiton atrosanguineum*) – mauve and purple fuchsia-like blooms **HHP/HHA**
Sweet peas – dwarf varieties, various colours **HA**

## Floppers and trailers
*Convolvulus minor* (syn. *C. tricolor*) – creeping plants with large pink, blue or mauve flowers often 'flashed' in another colour **HA**
*Nemophila maculata* – pale blue, single flowers with dark blue spot on tip of each petal **HA**
*Phacelia campanularia* – deep blue, bell-shaped flowers **HA**
Poached egg plant (*Limnanthes douglasii*) bright yellow petals edged white, bees love them **HA**
Swan river daisy (*Brachycome*) – purple daisy-like flowers **HHA**
Swiss balcony geraniums – flowers red, pink, white etc, narrow petals but plants are smothered in flower all summer **HHP**

## Delicate exotics
Hyacinth bean (*Dolichos lablab*) – climber with white or mauve flowers, 7.5cm/3in pods, beans used in oriental cookery **HHA**
*Lampranthus* – spreading 'ice plant', brightly coloured flowers only open in sun **HHP**
*Lantana camara* – balls of flower change colour from yellow to red as they open, gets lots of whitefly **HHP**
*Mina lobata* – climber, long sprays of white, yellow,

peach and red flowers, all occurring on the same stem **HHP/HHA**
Petunia, double frilly varieties – flowers like powder puffs in various colours, needs protection **HHA**
*Tweedia caerulea* – ice blue flowers, short climber, stiffish stems need tying in place on basket sides and chains for best display **HHP**

## Conservatory basket plants
*Asparagus sprengeri* – long trailing evergreen branches **GP**
*Browallia* – blue, bell-shaped flowers in summer or winter depending on sowing time **GA**
*Ceropegia woodii* (hearts entwined) – delicate, trailing plant, small heart-shaped, spotted leaves on thread-like stems, flowers insignificant **GP**
Creeping fig *(Ficus pumila)* – evergreen plant, rounded leaves on creeping stems; variegated version also available **IP**
Wax plant *(Hoya bella)* – evergreen leaves, floppy branching stems with clusters of red centred pale pink flowers in summer **IP**
*Petrea volubis* – climber with feathery sprays of star-like blue flowers, train stems out round basket and up chains for best display **GP**
*Stephanotis* – large, oval-leaved, twining climber with scented white flowers, train out round basket and up chains **IP**
*Thunbergia grandiflora* – climber with large, single blue flowers **GP**
Wishbone flowers (*Torenia fournieri*) – striking flowers, blue-grey and mauve with yellow throats, compact lax plants **GA**

## For fragrance
Scented-leaved pelargoniums – various scents including citrus, spices, pine, rose and so on, many varieties naturally floppy, plants nothing special to look at but release scent when touched **GP**

## Fillers
Arrowhead ivy (*Hedera helix* 'Sagittifolia') – long, elegant, deep green leaves **HP**
Mind your own business (*Helxine*) – masses of minute frothy foliage, green, gold or silver variegated varieties **HHP**

*For a striking show that changes colour as it flowers, try planting exotic* Lantana camara *(left) in a hanging basket. Its yellow balls of flowers turn red as they open.*

*Year-round indoor greenery can be provided by the delicate trailing fronds of* Asparagus sprengeri *(right) which makes an elegant addition to a conservatory. Other indoor evergreens worth experimenting with include the creeping fig (*Ficus pumila*) and the white-flowered* Stephanotis.

Harry Smith

*A single splash of colour creates a striking focal point as these pelargoniums show (right). They also demonstrate how effective the new ball of bloom baskets are.*

*A mixture of trailing and climbing plants in two or more harmonizing colours (below), such as the white, pink and purple flowers pictured here, creates a lovely, restful centrepiece for the garden.*

Andrew Lawson

Ron Sutherland/Garden Picture Library

Photos Horticultural

Hanging basket trees are invaluable if you do not have much room, as they look very decorative. By using plenty of cascading plants, you can create a sensational waterfall effect. But be sure to site hanging basket trees in a well sheltered position, so there is no risk of them blowing over.

## Ball of bloom basket

One of the newest hanging baskets on the market is designed to enable you to create a perfect ball of bloom. It consists of two halves of a hollow sphere which are filled with compost and then clipped together. Short planting tubes are set into the sides. Balls of bloom are only available from specialist suppliers and are not cheap. But you can create something similar yourself that costs much less.

Take two ordinary wire hanging baskets of the same size. Line each with moss, and slightly overfill them with gently firmed compost. (This is important or the compost will settle and leave the finished 'ball' empty at the top.)

Lay a thin sheet of plywood over one basket and hold it tightly while upturning this basket on top of the second. Slide the sheet of wood out, and fix the baskets firmly together with wire. Stand the basket on a bucket, which acts as a turntable for planting. Then push small plants in evenly over all the basket surface. Plant the base of the basket when it is hanging up. Make sure you secure it to a firm bracket, as by using two baskets you have effectively doubled its weight.

## Planting schemes

Even when using plants you are not familiar with, follow the same guidelines as for making a good traditional basket. Either use plants of all one type, perhaps in a mixture of colours for a formal basket, or take a mixture of tall climbing plants, plus shorter and

close together. Choose matching baskets of different sizes and hang them at different heights. Three or five baskets always look better grouped together than an even number. Or try hanging two or three baskets, one above the other on separate brackets, ranging in size from small to large, with the smallest at the top.

Plant a group of baskets so that while each basket looks different, there is some common link, such as the colour scheme, or one type of plant repeated throughout. Or you could fill one basket with climbers, another with trailers and a third with small spreading plants, placing them so close together they create one merging display.

## Hanging basket tree

A hanging basket tree is a stand that looks rather like an old fashioned hat stand, with curved arms from which you can suspend three or four baskets. You can also buy two-tiered versions, which allow you to hang baskets at two different levels.

Derek Gould

trailing types for a contrast.

In a conservatory or sun-room, half hardy perennial trailers are usually grown one kind per basket, which allows them to develop into large, spectacular specimens that fill the basket. If you want a mixed 'indoor' basket, choose species that have similar requirements and growth rates, or some will thrive at the expense of others.

### Plants

Try to include at least one self-twining climber in a mixed basket. This will climb up the chains of the basket creating a fuller display. Short but floppy plants look best grown in hanging baskets.

Slightly exotic annuals are best grown in a very sheltered spot, under the eaves, or in a porch where their delicate flowers are protected from the elements. Green creeping 'filler' plants are useful anywhere, making a good background to colourful flowers.

Photos Horticultural

*A bonus for the garden where space is at a premium, this two-tiered hanging basket tree (left) can be used to great decorative effect. Or simply hang a basket of white blooms in a tree (right) to create a cool contrast with the dark green foliage.*

*Self-twining climbers such as these black-eyed Susans (Thunbergia alata 'Susie Mixed') will in time grow up the chains of the basket for a lush spread (below left).*

*A hanging basket of tomatoes (below) is a practical solution for the very small garden, combining as it does colour and edibility.*

Peter McHoy

Photos Horticultural

Use them as 'living moss' either on the top surface of the basket, or all round in the case of the traditional wire kind.

And be adventurous with your choice of plants. Do not be afraid to try something new. Many exciting kinds are available if you experiment with growing your own from seed.

## PEST CONTROL

If hanging baskets are attacked by greenfly or whitefly, it can be very difficult to get rid of them owing to the dense foliage filling the basket. For best results use a pressure sprayer (buy a systemic pesticide and dilute with water following the manufacturer's instructions).

Set the nozzle to produce a fairly powerful blast which will reach between the outer leaves, allowing the product to coat all parts of the plants. Rotate the basket slightly as you spray to ensure even coverage. Take indoor or under-cover baskets out of doors to spray them; have a spare hanging bracket handy.

*GARDEN NOTES*

*Bearing colourful flowers almost continuously in the summer, pelargoniums are a popular choice for window boxes and are a common sight in the summer in many parts of Europe (above). Window boxes can, however, also present the gardener with many opportunities for creativity (left).*

# Wonderful Window Boxes

## With a little imagination you can improve the look of your place – from inside and out – by adding a window box of flowers or delightful foliage plants.

Neil Holmes

The most memorable window boxes are those that appear to cascade with colour and detail, with the container so hidden by foliage and flowers that it looks as if the plants are growing in the air.

To achieve this sort of effect you actually need to exercise restraint. When you first plant it the box will look a little sparse – but give it just a few weeks (and some water and fertilizer) and the plants will develop well.

Lobelia, verbena and trailing pelargoniums are some of the best choices for cascades of colour and texture. For height and spread use petunias or pansies. Tiny blue kingfisher daisies (*Felica bergeriana*) add a delicate touch to such a scheme with their feathery foliage. Trails of silver-leaved helichrysum or variegated ivy will complete the picture.

Whatever you choose to fill your window box, make sure that the box itself is secure on your window sill. If the sill slopes downwards, place two or three wooden wedges under

*Twin white window boxes perfectly set off this arrangement of red, white and pink flowers, amid varying shades of green foliage. This late summer display is dominated by the large red floral clusters of pelargoniums. The ivy will provide year-round interest.*

box to prevent it slipping.

If your windows open outwards you will need to fix the window box below the window sill. Fix it at least 30cm/12in lower than the sill, so that tall plants will keep their heads when the window is opened.

### Materials

Window boxes are available in a range of sizes and different materials.

**Terracotta** boxes look very attractive but you must be sure that they are frost-proof if winters are severe in your area. They lose water very quickly, so you must be prepared to check regularly that the soil hasn't dried out: in hot weather this may mean twice a day. They are relatively expensive.

**Wooden** boxes need to be treated against rot. Choose a wood preservative that will not be harmful to the plants in the box. As an extra precaution, line the sides of the box with plastic to prevent water getting into the wood from the inside.

**Plastic** window boxes are

## WINDOW BOX WATCHPOINTS

- Make sure the window box site is accessible so you can plant and maintain it through the year. Once a window box is planted up it will be too heavy to move.
- If you are working from inside the house, lay down newspaper on the floor inside the window and have ready a rubbish bag for any prunings, dead plants or waste compost.
- Always check that the compost is well watered, especially in summer.
- Feed window box plants with a liquid fertilizer during their flowering seasons.
- If there is no one to water your plants when you are on holiday, trail a capillary mat from a bucket of water and bury the other end in the compost. Water will be taken up gradually by the plants. Water the box well before you go away, so that the matting is drenched.

*Crocuses (above) provide early spring colour. Narcissi (below) produce another dash of spring colour in a box that will have looked good all winter, with its mix of evergreens.*

the front of the box, to level it. To be absolutely sure that the box is safe you should fix brackets to the wall on either side and one underneath the sill. Each bracket should protrude across the front of the

*Pink and red pelargoniums in full summer bloom (left) produce a lovely mound of eye-catching colour. Like all such arrangements, they look their best when set off by a neatly painted window box – white is always a good choice. A regular wash or a wipe with a cloth will keep the box and the window frames looking good.*

probably the best buy for all-year use. Modern plastics are durable – they don't crack in sunshine and are frost-proof. Once again you must keep an eye on the plants and water them frequently. Drainage holes are usually marked on the base of the box, but you will have to open them using a hand drill. Drip trays are usually bought separately. They hold excess moisture and stop water draining down over your window ledge.

### Window box maintenance
To make your window box plants perform well, *you* have to do a bit of work. In the

---

### PLANTING A SPRING BOX
Choose from your favourite spring flowers and create a winter-into-spring window box plan (right). You can achieve garden-like results in the small space of your window box.

**1** *Drainage is important, otherwise plants will rot. If you are using a container without drainage holes, such as a plastic trough, bore holes in the base of it.*

**2** *Add a layer of crocks to the bottom of your window box to improve drainage. Broken flowerpots are ideal. Since water passes quickly through them, plants will not be sitting in a pool of stagnant water. Crocks also prevent compost from blocking the drainage holes.*

**3** *On top of the crocks add a loamy, soil-based compost. If your window box has no drainage holes, a bulb compost, designed for such situations, can be mixed in with the main compost. For the best results, window boxes should be re-filled each year with fresh compost.*

**4** *Before planting up, remove any dead or dying leaves from your plants. Plant ivies in the front of the box to provide different shades and textures of green in winter and daffodils behind for early spring flowering. Water the box well.*

Steven Wooster/Garden Picture Library

Eric Crichton

Marshall Cavendish

S & O Mathews

ground a plant's roots search for water and food, but in a container the amount of water and nutrient in the soil depends on you. You need to replenish the water constantly, particularly in very hot weather and if the window box is in full sun all day.

Nutrients must be given fairly often. Give your plants a good start by setting them into a loamy, soil-based compost such as John Innes No 2. Peat composts dry out very quickly and have little nutrient material in them. During the growing and flowering season water the box with a liquid fertilizer every fortnight.

When you are planting up the box place a layer of stones or terracotta crocks in the base to improve drainage. The deeper your box, the taller and larger the plants you can grow

in it. For best effects, and if your window sill will hold it, a box 90cm/3ft long x 22cm/9in deep x 25cm/10in wide, is a good size to work with.

## A choice of plants

There is a huge variety of plants that you can choose for window box planting schemes. Obviously you can't grow every garden plant in a window box, but you can have a good deal of creative fun choosing the style, colour scheme and shape that your window box collection will have.

With window box gardens you can dress your windows throughout the year with sea-

*If your walls are covered with ivy or Virginia creeper, these plants will provide the ideal backdrop for a bright display in a window box. Pink and white petunias have been used (above) to good effect.*

*A single-colour theme, using various plants, can be very striking. Taking yellow as the theme, this window box (below) has been planted with chrysanthemums, broom (Cytisus) and variegated ivy. Other single-colour arrangements can be equally effective.*

sonal favourites that can be removed when they are past their best, replacing them with choice flowers and plants from the following season.

For a permanent framework use evergreen foliage plants and conifers. Variegated ivy, available in a wide range of creamy white and yellow-green combinations, will provide trailing swags of background colour. The ivy trails will also soften and diguise the look of the window box.

*Euonymus fortunei* 'Emerald Gaiety', an evergreen, upright and bushy shrub, offers cream and green foliage that takes on a rosy tint in autumn. Dwarf conifers come in a range

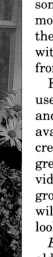

---

### WINDOW BOX THEMES

- **Herb box**: Upright rosemary, sage, thyme and salad burnet offer a good range of colour, shape and flowers.
- **Salad box 1**: 'Tom Thumb' lettuce, clumps of chives and 'Pixie' tomatoes will provide shape, colour and produce.
- **Salad box 2**: Sow cut-and-come-again red and green lettuce in the front of the box and 'Pixie' tomatoes at the back.
- **Spring box**: Plant *Alyssum saxatile* in front to trail over the edge of the box; grape hyacinth bulbs in the next row and dwarf tulips such as *Tulipa greigii* hybrids at the back of the window box.
- **Cascade box**: Trailing fuchsias, ivy-leaved pelargoniums, variegated ground ivy, verbena and trailing lobelia.
- **Up-and-down-box**: For a cascade combined with an upright effect, grow 'Knee-Hi' sweet peas at the back of the box with trailing ivy-leaved pelargoniums in the middle of the box. For trailing foliage use ivy.

*BRIGHT IDEAS*

---

### POSSIBLE PROBLEMS

- Brown or shrivelled leaves are signs of lack of water or of wind burn in winter. In winter, water only sparingly, as the compost will not dry out so quickly.
- Aphids can cause trouble. Spray the plants with soapy water from time to time when you see signs of insect damage.

*GARDEN NOTES*

of silver, grey and golden colours. They add height and shape to a display.

## Brightening it up

In between these framework plants you can add winter and spring colour by planting winter-flowering pansies and spring-flowering bulbs and primulas. When the bulbs and spring flowers are finished, remove them and add your favourite summer bedding plants. With such a planting scheme your box always has a basic shape and height, with bright colours each season.

*A herb garden in a window box is both useful and attractive. It can be planted up (right) with such herbs as mint, parsley, chives and fennel. Nasturtiums and violas will add colour, while mint and chives can be left to flower.*

Andrew Lawson

## PLANTS FOR WINDOW BOXES

| Flower | Colours | Height | Season |
|---|---|---|---|
| Crocus | yellow, purple cream | 8cm/3in | spring |
| Grape hyacinth (Muscari) | blue, white | 18cm/7in | spring |
| Heathers (Erica carnea) | purple, pink, white | 25cm/10in | winter |
| Pansies | mixed colours | 15-20cm/6-8in | summer or winter |
| Swan river daisy | blue | 20-25cm/8-10in | summer/autumn |
| Busy Lizzie (Impatiens) | red, pinks, striped | 15-25cm/6-10in | summer |
| *Tulipa greigii* | red, yellow, cream | 25cm/10in | late spring |
| Petunias (dwarf varieties) | pastels, deep reds, blues, doubles | 20-30cm/8-12in | summer/autumn |
| Wallflowers (dwarf varieties) | yellows, orange, dark red | 30cm/12in | spring |
| French marigold (Tagetes patula) | orange, yellow, red, mahogany | 15-30cm/6-12in | summer/autumn |
| Sweet Pea 'Bijou mixed' | mixed | 30cm/12in | summer |
| **Trailing plants** | | | |
| Lobelia | blue, white, mauve | 15cm/6in trailing | summer/autumn |
| *Alyssum saxatile* | yellow | 20cm/8in cascading | spring |
| Verbena | mixed | 25cm/10in trailing | summer/autumn |
| Ivy-leafed pelargonium | pinks, mauves, some with variegated foliage | 25cm/10in trailing foliage | summer/autumn |
| Nasturtium 'Alaska' | orange, yellow, cream-variegated foliage | 30cm/12in trailing | summer/autumn |
| Nasturtium 'Gleam hybrids' | orange, yellow | 30cm/12in trailing | summer/autumn |
| **Foliage plants** | | | |
| Ivy | green, white, creamy yellow | trailing | all year round |
| Helichrysum | silvery foliage | trailing | all year in mild areas |
| Ground ivy | variegated green and white | trailing | all year in mild areas |

You can make an all-year herb window box. For the framework of permanent plants, use perennial herbs like sage and thyme. Add nasturtiums and marigolds in summer for colour. (Their petals can be added to summer salads.) Chives and salad burnet also have attractive flowers and their leaves are invaluable in salads.

For an aromatic window box, use lavender or hyssop. Harvest the flowers and leaves of lavender to use in pot pourri or in fragrant drawer bags. You can use the hyssop leaves to add aromatic oils to a bath or as a herbal tea.

Single-colour schemes work well in a window box. In winter use white or purple heathers planted closely like a miniature flowering hedge. Keep them in their individual pots (they like acid soil conditions) and plant bulbs of complementary colours around the heathers. In spring you will then have a fresh look for the window box. Later you can remove the heathers and bulbs and replant the whole box with a summer scheme.

### Creating a natural look

Bring a natural look to your spring window box by using alpines and bulbs. *Alyssum saxatile* grows to form a grey carpet and is a perfect companion for a mass of crocuses.

# Winter Window Boxes

**Cold weather need not bring your window box displays to an end. Arrangements of colourful foliage and flowers will brighten up winter window-sills.**

Jon Bouchier/Garden Picture Library

There are a number of ways of achieving successful winter displays. One of the simplest is to use box liners that you can slip in and out of your window box. These liners, usually made of recycled cellulose, allow you to prepare an attractive arrangement of plants in advance.

You can plant up box liners with winter-flowering bulbs, pansies or primulas. As soon as summer plants are past their best they can be removed and can be replaced by the already planted and partially established winter containers. Use two or three to fill a box; a larger size would be too heavy to move when planted up.

At the end of the flowering season the liners can be placed in a less obvious part of the garden to allow bulb foliage to die back naturally.

*An arrangement of evergreens (above), enlivened by the deep pink blooms of cyclamen. The small shrub with leaves dotted yellow is spotted laurel (Aucuba japonica), a versatile permanent plant for window boxes. Grow both male and female plants if you want red berries from autumn to spring. There are a number of varieties.*

Harry Smith Collection

Peter McHoy

Another option is to include in your window box some permanent plants that look good the whole year round.

### Permanent framework

A design based around evergreens allows you to fill in the spaces between them each season with appropriate colourful flowers. Heathers, ivies and miniature conifers and evergreen shrubs are ideal permanent plants.

Foliage need never be dull. Conifers and heathers have foliage in shades of green or in red, gold or bronze. Many evergreen shrubs and ivies have colourful variegated leaves.

Conifers come in a wide variety of shapes, from slim spires to globes. Some form squat cushions and there are ground-covering forms that hang over box edges. Together with low, spreading heathers and trailing, evergreen creepers, there is no shortage of shapes to choose from.

Creating a skeleton design from evergreens keeps work and expense to a minimum.

### Evergreens in pots

If you prefer to remove all the summer plants and replace them at the onset of winter, grow a few evergreens in pots. Sink them into the compost in your box and plant bulbs and flowering plants around them.

*A simple design (above left) of upright blue-green conifers with variegated Euonymus fortunei and ivy. If you have little or no window-sill, a window box should be attached securely to the wall just below the window.*

*The window box itself can add a splash of colour (above right) to brighten up a window-sill. This one has a black steel framework with red ceramic tiles.*

*The white flowers of heather and viola (below) complement a cream and green hebe and contrast well with the dark greens of a cypress and ivy.*

Working to a shape creates the best effect. If the view from your window is pleasing use a swag arrangement to provide a decorative frame.

### Designing a shape

Suitable plants for the box ends would be two slim, column-shaped conifers, such as young *Chamaecyparis lawsoniana* 'Elwoodii', which has attractive grey-green foliage.

A compact, globe-shaped *Cryptomeria japonica* 'Compressa', which has green foliage, tinted red-purple in winter, could go next. Plant winter-flowering heathers in the centre, with ivy or periwinkle trailing over the edge.

If you prefer a less symmetrical design, place two tall, slim conifers at one end. *Picea glauca albertina* 'Conica', for

Juliette Wade/Garden Picture Library

---

### FIRM FIXINGS

Winter winds make it especially important that boxes are securely fixed. Use wall plugs and screws to fix brackets to the wall, and where possible, screw the brackets to the base of the box. For added safety screw a hook to the wall either side of the window and fix large screw eyes in both ends of the box. Run thick wire or a chain between each hook and screw eye.

*SAFETY FIRST*

instance, makes a compact green pyramid. Then add smaller, dome-shaped types towards the centre and include one medium-sized spherical conifer at the opposite end.

Partially hide an ugly view with variegated ivy trained on wires fixed across the lower half of the window. In summer, add flowering climbers like nasturtiums or the unusual canary creeper (*Tropaeolum peregrinum*).

If you want to use tall plants in a box without obstructing the view, you should fix the box to the wall below sill level.

## Colour schemes

As winter-flowering window box plants are seen in the main from inside the house they look most effective if they tie in with the room's decoration. Alternatively, go for a

*An attractive terracotta box (right) sets off the cascading stems of a variegated ivy. White violas add floral appeal.*

Tommy Candler/Garden Picture Library

| SLOW-GROWING CONIFERS | | |
|---|---|---|
| **Type and habit** | **Foliage colour** | **Approx maximum size** |
| **Ground cover forms** | | |
| *Juniperus chinensis* 'Pfitzerana Aurea'. Low, prostrate form | golden | 150cm/60in spread |
| *J. conferta conferta.* Carpeter | silver on underside | 90cm/36in spread |
| *J. squamata* 'Blue Star'. Forms compact mound | silvery blue | 60cm/24in spread |
| **Pyramid forms** | | |
| *Chamaecyparis obtusa* 'Nana Aurea'. Foliage in twisted whorls | golden | 60cm/24in height |
| *C. pisifera* 'Plumosa Pygmaea'. Cone-shaped bush | golden | 90cm/36in height |
| *Juniperus communis* 'Compressa'. Compact spire shape | grey-green | 45cm/18in height |
| *Picea glauca* 'Nana'. Bush shape | grey-blue | 90cm/36in height |
| *Thuja occidentalis* 'Rheingold'. Fine, feathery foliage | soft gold turning bronze in winter | 100cm/40in height |
| **Globe-shaped forms** | | |
| *Chamaecyparis pisifera* 'Compacta Variegata'. Low bun shape | golden | 60cm/24in height |
| *Thuja occidentalis* 'Globosa'. Small dense globe | strong green | 45cm/18in height |
| *T. orientalis* 'Aurea Nana'. Egg-shaped bush | bright gold-green turning bronze in winter | 60cm/24in height |
| *T. orientalis* 'Minima Glauca'. Miniature globe | blue-green | 30cm/12in height |
| *T. orientalis* 'Rosedalis'. Upright oval | summer:green/winter: purple/spring: yellow | 60cm/24in height |

NOTE: Most of these conifers will only grow 1-2cm/½-1in per year.

contrast by choosing sunny colours against the background of a room with a cool white, green or blue interior.

**A golden scheme** can be based around the gold-tinted conifers shown in the chart. Add yellow-flushed ivies like *Hedera helix* 'Goldheart', which has yellow centres to its leaves, or *H. h.* 'Buttercup',

## COLOURFUL PANSIES

The pansy is one of the best winter-flowering plants. Universal pansies come in a huge range of clear plain colours and in two-colour effects, as well as in white.

The garden pansy *Viola × wittrockiana* comes in winter-flowering as well as summer-flowering types and will flower through the winter in milder areas.

*BRIGHT IDEAS*

Jon Bouchier/Garden Picture Library

Jon Bouchier/Garden Picture Library

which has new leaves of bright yellow that soften to pale green later.

Choose bulbs like winter aconite (*Eranthis hyemalis*) which, in late winter, has buttercup-coloured flowers surrounded by a ruff of green bracts. Or you could plant the yellow, early-spring-flowering crocus, *Crocus chrysanthus* 'E.A. Bowles'.

**For a silver and white scheme** pick variegated *Euonymus fortunei* 'Silver Queen', a shrub with green leaves edged in creamy white. Add white heathers, particularly the varieties of *Erica herbacea* (also sold as *E. carnea*). *E. h.* 'Cecilia M. Beale' blooms from early winter, while *E. h.* 'Springwood White' flowers vigorously from late winter.

Among the many ivies go for *Hedera helix* 'Silver Queen' with its green and silver leaves, or, in a sheltered situation, *H. h.* 'Eva' which has delightfully small, grey-green

*Skimmias are hardy, evergreen shrubs, ideal for winter window boxes. They are usually grown for their bright clusters of red berries (above). One variety has red-brown flower buds (top right) in autumn and winter, which add subtle variety to this box of evergreens and colourful cyclamens, though this type of cyclamen is not frost-hardy.*

leaves edged with cream.

There is little to rival the heart-warming emergence of snowdrops. *Galanthus elwesii* has large flowers that appear in late winter.

**A blue and pink scheme** could include the blue-green conifers and the ivy *H. helix* 'Tricolor', which has white-bordered leaves that turn a deep pink in autumn.

Several varieties of frost hardy cyclamen flower in autumn, winter or early spring.

The bright pink flowers of *Cyclamen coum*, for instance, appear in early winter. There are also many different pink heathers to choose from.

### Winter care
As most window boxes are sheltered from the rain by the house wall, they will need watering often, even in winter. Conifers, in particular, require moist conditions, as do pansies and primulas. If frost is expected, do not water until conditions turn warmer.

Winter-flowering plants need feeding but for most plants winter is a time of rest. Feed the plants in your winter box once, a few weeks after planting, then just once or twice in spring.

Extreme cold winds can damage the foliage of even hardy plants. It is worth protecting your box in severe frost or snow with a covering of sacking. House walls offer some protection. In extreme cold, the city dweller, surrounded by warm buildings, has the advantage over those living in the country.

# Shrubs in Tubs

**If it's a formal look you're after, clipped bay trees by the front door, shaped yew on the patio, and upright conifers on the balcony will add a touch of class to even the smallest garden.**

Eric Crichton

Formal shrubs in tubs do not belong only in grand gardens. They are often at their most effective in relatively modest spaces where they have lots of impact. In a very small town garden, a patio, balcony or roof garden, a few formal container shrubs will add welcome greenery and real character.

Many informal shrubs – those with a loose outline or spreading profile, such as Japanese maples and false castor oil plant – make excellent container shrubs. It is the crisp, geometric outline of formal shrubs, however, that makes them especially useful as focal-point plants or for creating a sense of design and structure in a garden.

### Bold statements

You can, of course, grow formal shrubs in the ground, but planted among other shrubs they often lose some of their impact, and you cannot move them around at will, as you can when they are in containers.

You can place these potted shrubs where their very unexpectedness is an attraction – by the front porch, or on a balcony for instance.

### Pot panache

The containers, too, make a vital contribution. By raising a shrub off the ground and presenting it in splendid isolation, they actually enhance the plant. As formal shrubs are usually evergreen, and most will be grown for foliage effect, a container that has a bold or intricate design will add another element of interest.

*Clay pots (far left), painted to match the front door, make ideal containers for the variegated Aucuba japonica 'Maculata'. The effect is stylish yet unimposing and provides the finishing touch to an enclosed porch.*

*These bay trees (right) have been trained into tall columns and are being used to frame an unusual arched window. The stylish elegance is reflected in the smart white painted wooden 'Versailles' tubs.*

*For a less constrained, yet still formal approach, this bay tree has been left to grow naturally. The softer outline compliments the country charm of the cottage.*

Eric Crichton

### CONTAINER TIPS

● Check the maximum size of the shrub before planting; you don't want a plant which will block the light from windows or which will look too large for the pot.

● As container plants use up nutrients quickly, nourish them occasionally with a liquid feed during the summer according to the manufacturer's instructions.

● With established plants, remove the top 2.5–5cm/1–2in of soil each spring and replace it with a good loam-based compost.

*DON'T FORGET!*

Eric Crichton

For quick and dependable results, keep to widely available, reliable plants to achieve the desired effect.

### What to grow

**Bay** (*Laurus nobilis*) responds well to formal clipping, and is ideal to use in pairs by the front or back door. There is also the bonus of bay leaves for the kitchen – but do not raid the plant too often or you will spoil its shape.

There is just one major drawback with bay; it is not reliably hardy. In mild areas, it will survive most winters unharmed, but it is not a good choice in cold districts, especially as container plants are more vulnerable to frosts.

**Box** (*Buxus sempervirens*) thrives on formal clipping, and is really tough. You can buy ready-clipped pyramids from good nurseries and garden centres, though you will still have to keep it trimmed.

If you want to train your own (which is much cheaper), buy a tall-growing variety. 'Handsworthensis' is a good one, or choose the variegated 'Aureovariegata' for a lighter, more colourful look.

**Privet** is cheap, tough, and quick-growing – all of which makes it a good one to try if you want to start training your own plants. You will need to clip it frequently as it can become unruly, and it lacks the elegance that some of the more 'classic' plants possess, but a golden privet will bring colour to a dull corner in a way that other traditional green formal shrubs cannot.

**Shrubby honeysuckle** (*Lonicera nitida*), not to be confused with the climbing group of honeysuckles, is another inexpensive plant that clips well to a formal shape. It is unlikely that these will be available as ready-trained specimens, but they are widely sold as hedging plants, and it is easy to clip them to almost any shape. There is a golden form that is particularly attractive, 'Baggesen's Gold'.

### Cutting style

**Yew** is a favourite topiary plant, but it does not generally do so well as a container plant. You can, however, sometimes buy ready trained container-

29

Ron Sutherland/The Garden Picture Library

*It is worth standing a particularly fine specimen of a tender shrub such as this Heptapleureum arboricola 'Variegata' (above) on the patio for the summer. Keep such plants indoors during the winter months or they will be killed by frosts.*
*A sleek conifer (right) with its tall, narrow shape creates a distinctive focal point near a window or doorway. This easy-to-care-for shrub makes it a practical choice.*

Andrew Lawson

*The beauty of this euonymus fortunei 'Emerald and Gold' (left) lies in its delicately patterned foliage. Colourful all year round, it is the perfect addition to a patio, path, balcony or any area that needs brightening up. It can be trimmed into shape using shears if a more formal look is desired.*

Harry Smith Collection

grown topiary specimens.

If you want to experiment, and save money at the same time, start with something easy to train like a holly or the winter-flowering bushy ever-green *Viburnum tinus*.

You are unlikely to buy these ready-trained, but if you do not mind waiting a few years, the results will be im-pressive (hollies in particular can be very slow growing). Both of these plants are widely available in garden centres.

To keep faster growing for-mal shrubs in shape, clip them with shears as frequently as necessary – this may be as much as several times in one growing season.

Plants with larger leaves

Harry Smith Collection

*Box (left) is the ideal shrub for clipping and this one has been trimmed into a lovely ball shape. The simplicity of the pot complements the rounded outlines. Similarly, this beautiful bay (right) has been trained into an ellipse and its formal oval outline contrasts well with the easy country charm of a wooden barrel.*

*Cupressus macrocarpa (below) is an excellent choice as a container shrub. Fast growing and aromatic, it does not require frequent clipping.*

## FIVE FAVOURITES

- Box (*Buxus sempervirens*). Small, leathery, dark green leaves. Variegated varieties available. Easily clipped.

- Bay (*Laurus nobilis*). Large, leathery green leaves. The beauty lies in the formal shaping. Trained specimens are widely available.

- Privet (*ligustrum*). Try a golden variety for a brighter look. Easily clipped to shape.

- Shrubby honeysuckle (*Lonicera nitida*). Small green leaves, and quick growth. Easy to train; but requires frequent clipping.

- Yew (*taxus baccata*). Tolerates close clipping.

*GARDEN NOTES*

Derek Gould

should not be clipped with shears, however.

The least expensive choice for a grow-your-own formal container plant is a conifer. Many grow naturally into an attactive oval or cone, without any trimming. Because many are relatively quick-growing, they are also usually inexpensive. You can buy fairly large container-grown specimens for much less than you would pay for other trained evergreens of similar size. They need not be boring either: try golden forms, or those with unusual blue-grey foliage.

Not all conifers do well in containers, however. Some cannot tolerate dry roots, which is a hazard for container plants if you forget to water regularly in dry spells.

### Choosing containers

A generous amount of good compost is essential if your shrub is to thrive in a container. Similarly good drainage is a must. Some plastic shrub tubs come with areas of

### SHAPING UP

**Pencil column**

**Pyramid shape**

**'Lollipop'**

**Oval outline**

Buy plants ready-trained for stunning effects. Use shears for small leaved plants and secateurs for larger leaves.

thin plastic that have to be punched out to create drainage holes. Any container which is less than 30cm/12in in diameter is unlikely to be suitable for a tree or shrub; ideally 45cm/18in is the minimum size unless the plant is still very small.

**Plastic** tubs are practical and inexpensive but generally do not look very imposing.

**Imitation stone** (sometimes known as reconstituted stone) is very impressive and an ornamental pot or urn, perhaps with some ornate decoration, or standing on a plinth, is just right for a plant such as a formal clipped bay or a neat specimen conifer.

**Frost-proof clay** or terracotta pots come in wide variety of shapes and sizes and are ideal for shrubs cut into 'lollipops' or similar shapes as their simplicity will enhance rather than detract from the overall effect.

**Wooden 'Versailles'** tubs, square in shape, are elegant and look especially good containing bay pyramids. Some plastic versions can look very convincing.

**Half barrels** make ideal shrub tubs. Before you plant anything in them ensure that they have suitable drainage by

## POT TRAINING

**Q** I have had a clipped bay for several years but some of the leaves look brown at the edges.

**A** The brown leaves are probably the result of winter cold or wind burn if it stands in a windy or exposed position. Move it to a sheltered spot, especially in winter.

**Q** I have a conifer in a pot and would like to add some seasonal colour. Can I plant something else in the container?

**A** Try a few small spring-flowering bulbs such as crocuses or grape hyacinths, and a small trailing variegated ivy. Unless the pot is very large, however, summer bedding plants may be deprived of moisture so water daily. Dead-head flowers for a long summer display.

*WHAT WENT WRONG?*

drilling a few large holes in the bottom. You may like to paint them white, maybe with black hoops. These make attractive containers for most formal shrubs.

## PROJECT PLANTING A SHRUB

1. Place a thick layer of crocks or large gravel in the bottom of the container to improve drainage, remembering that it must also have drainage holes.
2. Add a good loam-based compost to a depth that will bring the root-ball to within about 5cm/2in of the rim of the container. Don't depend on the garden soil. Container plants use a lot of nutrients and the soil probably won't have enough to feed the plant.
3. Remove the shrub from its container, tease out a few large roots, and trickle compost around until it is level with the top of the root-ball. Water well.

Tania Midgley

*To prevent weeds, sprinkle a layer of gravel around the top.*

# Rhododendrons and Azaleas in Tubs

**The many varieties of rhododendron and azalea can flower in winter, spring or summer. Dramatic when in bloom, they always look good in containers.**

Have you ever wished your display of plants in pots and containers would go on right through the year, with at least something green to look at during the depths of winter?

One way of achieving this is to grow rhododendrons or azaleas in containers. You can then have rich colourful flowers in summer, and some good evergreen foliage through the winter. They make a perfect choice for containers in town gardens, and if you live on limy soil, either in town or country, this may be the only easy way for you to grow these lime-hating but spectacularly beautiful plants.

Remember that azaleas are just a particular kind of rhododendron. They are generally more delicate in appearance, with smaller flowers, and are often deciduous or semi-evergreen, but they can be grown in just the same way as the usually larger, evergreen rhododendrons.

### Good in pots

Rhododendrons are ideally suited to life in containers. They have attractive foliage all the year, some with small rounded leaves and others with long glossy ones. They make an even, domed shape which is very pleasing in a container, as is the more bowl-

*Azaleas (right) and rhododendrons make stunning container displays and are easy to care for.*

Harry Smith Collection

Harry Smith Collection

shaped outline of the rather smaller azaleas.

They all have shallow roots which can be easily accommodated in a pot, and there is no tap-root. They are not hungry plants and require little in the way of feeding.

There are, however, one or two aspects of life in a pot which rhododendrons do not relish. They need cool, shady soil, and do not like dry soil and heat around their roots.

Although they like a lot of

*Rhododendron 'Cowslip' (above) is a popular and easily available variety, with creamy-yellow flowers in early to mid spring.*

*The dramatic, glowing red blooms of R. 'Britannia' (right) have made it a gardener's favourite. Tough and wind-resistant, it is particularly well-suited to a container.*

*The imperial colour of R. 'Purple Splendour' (below) is unusual to find among rhododendrons. This variety, with attractive frilled flowers and a prominent black ray in the throat, flowers in late spring and early summer.*

Photos Horticultural

Photos Horticultural

water, they hate being waterlogged. Not all rhododendrons are hardy when their roots are in a container that is above the ground and exposed to the frost. Some extra protection is often a good idea.

### Buying your plants

Generally speaking, the tougher hybrid rhododendrons are most suitable for growing in containers.

The more tender species are better avoided, however elegant they may be.

Look for low densely-foliaged specimens with no hint of yellow in the leaves. You can choose root-balled or pot-grown plants.

It makes sense to buy your plants in spring when they will be ready to plant out in the new compost of a container. Pot-grown specimens can be planted into containers any time during the summer. If you buy a rhododendron in

## FEEDING

Rhododendrons and azaleas are not hungry plants and positively resent large doses of fertilizer. As long as they look healthy and flower well, resist the temptation to feed them regularly.

The best type of nourishment for a rhododendron is a top dressing of leaf mould in the spring, preferably enriched with a little bone meal.

Treating the plants with Sequestrene or a similar plant 'tonic' from time to time (but do not overdo this) will ensure that they get the trace elements, such as iron, that are necessary to healthy growth.

Photos Horticultural

winter, keep the plant in its existing pot, or in the ground, until you put it into its container in the spring.

### Composts

Ordinary potting compost – even peat-based ones – contain too much lime for most rhododendrons. You need to buy ericaceous compost, which is formulated especially for acid-loving plants like rhododendrons and heathers.

Work a little extra grit into the compost to keep it free-draining, and make the compost at the bottom of the pot very gritty. The grit, of course, must not be limestone. Use a layer of broken clay pots to cover the holes in the bottom of the container.

Leaf mould makes an excellent alternative to ericaceous compost, if you can get it, and should also be mixed with grit.

When planting your rhododendron, make sure you leave the soil level 4-5cm/1½-2in below the rim of the pot to allow for generous watering.

### Tubs

In choosing containers for rhododendrons, look for ones which are wider than they are high. A tub made from half a barrel is about right, although it would be far too big as a first pot for most new rhododendrons. However, any large wooden, stone, concrete or terracotta container makes a good home for these plants.

Plastic pots will do for rhododendrons, but they are not as good as terracotta or other tubs, even if they retain the moisture better.

### Growing on

Keep your containerized rhododendrons in a bright, sunny place during the summer, but one which is not too hot.

The tender indoor azaleas (*Rhododendron simsii*) can of course be plunged, in their pots, into garden soil for the summer in half shade, but must be brought indoors again before the autumn.

Most rhododendrons and azaleas make a good, even shape of their own accord, but it may be necessary on occasion to pinch out a tip or two, to make the plant bush out.

Gillian Beckett

*A fairly large and sturdy terracotta pot (left) is an ideal home for a container-grown rhododendron. Since a pot of this size and weight is not easy to move, choose a sunny but sheltered spot for the plant, to provide winter protection.*

*R. yakushimanum (right) is one of the best rhododendrons for containers, growing to a dome-shaped height of about 90cm/36in. Its pretty flowers are starkly white when open but deep pink in bud.*

*The Kurume hybrid azalea 'Amoenum' (below right), with striking magenta-pink flowers appearing in spring, is evergreen, thus providing winter interest.*

*R. 'Daviesii' (below), a deciduous Ghent azalea, is notable for its fragrant, creamy-white and yellow blotched flowers.*

Tania Midgley

Harry Smith Collection

Plants should be potted on every two or tree years. A good guide is the spread of the plant's foliage. When this is almost twice the width of the pot, then it is time to re-pot.

Like garden rhododendrons, most container-grown plants are not easily damaged by cold or frost. However, most will benefit from being placed in a position where they will be protected from the rays of the early morning sun.

## WATERING

*GROWING TIPS*

Rhododendrons and azaleas cannot tolerate lime in the soil, and it quickly turns the leaves a yellow colour.

When grown in containers they must be given soft water with no lime in it. If your tap water is limy, you will need to collect rainwater. Make sure the butt is well sealed to stop leaves getting into the water and souring it.

So long as you have got the drainage right, rhododendrons will enjoy generous watering. If you happen to let your container dry out, give it a good soaking to ensure that the rootball and compost are thoroughly wet.

In times of drought through the summer, you may have to use limy tap water on your rhododendrons, but make sure it is only for as short a period as possible.

Wall pots are an easy way to bring colour to your garden quickly and offer a wealth of opportunity for creativity. Ivy-leafed pelargonium, for example, has been planted in a manger with lobelia and fuchsia (above) to make a lax, informal display, while pansies, aubrieta and ivy (left) are combined to make a delightful half basket.

# Wall Pots and Baskets

**Wall-mounted pots and baskets introduce all sorts of attractive design and colour possibilities where space is at a premium.**

Whatever the size of your outside space, wall pots and baskets are an inventive way of decorating brickwork and wooden fences. They can be used to brighten up the outside of the house, or to enliven a balcony, patio or back yard. They will also improve the appearance of a shed or garage.

Wall pots and baskets differ from hanging baskets in that they fit flat against the wall, rather than hanging free. They come in a wide variety of materials and designs, ranging from the classical to the ultra-modern.

They are certainly not second best to hanging baskets and, in fact, have one important advantage. Hanging baskets must be regularly turned to prevent the display becoming one-sided. Wall pots and baskets, of course, are intended to be one-sided.

## Creating an effect

Like all containers, wall pots and baskets are invaluable for creating a splash of colour or a feeling of greenery in a very short space of time. Used in conjunction with window boxes, hanging baskets and floor level pots and troughs, they are the perfect addition to the container garden.

A bare expanse of white wall or brickwork is the ideal canvas for creating an individual arrangement. Rather than position the containers in a straight line, an informal effect can be achieved by stag-

*Wall pots and baskets, attached to a wall, fence or trellis, can be combined with hanging baskets for a really colourful display.*

Ann Kelly/Garden Picture Library

gering them down the wall in a series of steps. They also look pretty in groups of five or seven, giving the impression of a cascade of colour.

Wall pots look best at eye level or just above it. If you position them too high, the beauty of the pot and the plants within it will be lost.

### The right choice

When choosing a pot or basket you will find a wide range of materials and styles. Remember that they tend to be smaller in capacity than other containers, because of the flat back. Pick the largest ones you can find, as these will be the least likely to dry out. Wall baskets may need to be lined with sphagnum moss, though some are sold with fibre liners.

Think about the colour and texture of the wall surface. Brightly coloured plastics can look out of place, so go for neutral white or a natural shade of green to blend with the background and the plants.

Terracotta and stone look good against older materials

Insight Picture Library

Ron Sutherland/Garden Picture Library

Ron Sutherland/Garden Picture Library

*Hanging pots of purple petunias and white busy Lizzies (far left) have been skilfully arranged to conceal an unsightly drainpipe.*

*An ornate green wall pot neatly sets off a collection of evergreens on a stone-clad wall (left). Victorian pots like this were of cast iron but lightweight reproductions are available today. The plant with the bright fruits is Solanum pseudocapsicum 'Balloon'.*

*Four wall baskets, planted with petunias and nemesia, among other plants, form a swathe of colour on a plain fence (below left).*

*A basket of bright marigolds (below) contrasts effectively with a pale stone wall.*

Insight Picture Library

such as brick. Try setting a terracotta pot against a brilliant white wall for a sunny, mediterranean look. If your wall pots will be outside all year, check that the terracotta you buy is frost-proof.

It's also worth thinking about the weight that has to be supported. Plastic and wire mesh are the lightest materials, suitable for wooden fences or rendered walls. Small terracotta pots are not heavy either. Genuine antique stone pots should be treated with caution and only used where the structure of the wall is very solid. Reconstituted stone is usually lighter, but pick one up and check the weight before you buy.

### Different shapes

Most wall pots and baskets are half-moon shaped, rather like a hanging basket sliced in

### HANGING ORDINARY POTS

An easy and inexpensive way to create a large splash of colour is to put up a piece of heavy duty, plastic-coated steel mesh on a wall or fence. You can then hang groups of conventional plant pots on this and change the display regularly, as often as you like.

The pots are suspended using pot holders and simple metal kitchen hooks. The mesh must be securely fastened to the wall or fence using screw-in eyes.

**BRIGHT IDEAS**

half. If you hunt around the garden ornament sections of some garden centres you may also find other shapes such as the 'swallow's nest', which is

39

narrower and deeper.

Terracotta and reconstituted stone models are often adorned with garlands or raised motifs. These are attractive features but bear in mind before you choose that they may be entirely hidden if you are going to plant up the pots with a lot of trailing plants.

Many models have a hanging plate at the back with an 'eye' hole. The hole is designed to slip over a screw or a hook. The wall should be drilled, and the screw or hook firmly set using a wall-plug.

If you are fixing a wall pot to

Jerry Pavia/Garden Picture Library

Neil Holmes

*A pot or basket on a wall (above) allows you to add height and variety to any planting scheme, even in the smallest of areas. Here pink and red trailing pelargoniums cascade down.*

*Bright flowers, such as these pansies (right), are very striking against a light background. The pot tones in with the weathered brickwork.*

*Mounting pots on a wall covered with climbing and trailing plants (left) is a way to add variety. The variegated trailing plants in pots add a subtle element to this area of foliage. Colourful flowers would have a more dramatic impact.*

# PROJECT
## HOW TO PLANT A WALL BASKET

**1** Line the basket with damp sphagnum moss. The thicker the layer of moss, the less the basket will dry out.

**2** Bags of moss can be bought from garden centres but you could collect your own. Add a 5cm/2in layer of potting compost.

**3** Add trailing plants at the front and sides, pushing them through the basket mesh. Ensure the roots are embedded in the compost.

**4** Add more compost in layers, inserting more of your plants until the compost almost reaches the top of the moss.

**5** Finally, put non-trailing plants in the centre. Firm them down, cover bare compost with moss and water well.

a wooden fence, it is best to fix it to the strong upright posts. Do not position the pot above garden furniture or barbecue equipment, or anywhere where it could drip and cause annoyance.

### Planting up

When planting up your wall pots, the trick is to choose plants in scale with the pot rather than those that will swamp it. Avoid tall-growing species and choose the smaller trailing plants. Pelargonium 'L'Élégante', for instance, hangs prettily over the edge of a pot or basket.

For the centre of the pot, miniature bulbs are a good choice for spring and summer. Or use dwarf varieties of your favourite summer annuals. Small, mound-forming alpines are another possibility. Alpines, however, will need well-drained compost with a high proportion of grit or coarse sand.

Last but not least, don't forget herbs. Even if you do not plan to use them in the kitchen, parsley, creeping thyme and golden marjoram make a stunning display. Avoid herbs that grow too tall, such as sage and fennel.

The choice of colour schemes will depend on the situation and the effect you wish to achieve. You can be bold and mix plants in striking colours or go for a softer look with coordinated pastels. It is often effective to use just one species of plant in a wall pot. Vivid scarlet geraniums or a collection of ivies, for instance, look good on their own.

### Easy maintenance

Once planted, the care of wall pots and baskets is relatively simple. The most important thing is to keep them well-watered. With only a small reservoir of compost, they can dry out quickly in hot weather. If possible, water them daily in summer, less often at other seasons. A liquid feed every two weeks from spring to autumn will top up the nutrients.

Remove any dead flowers regularly. Wall pots and baskets are usually best replanted each year, before the plants get overgrown and leggy.

# Distinctive Containers

**Containers now come in all shapes, sizes and materials. Filled with a variety of attractive plants, they can add interest to every corner of the garden.**

The great beauty of containers is their versatility. They allow you to garden anywhere – even places where there is no soil. They are also the perfect way to personalize your garden without breaking the bank. You can stand containers on paths, by front and back doors, on balconies or flat roofs. Window boxes are wonderful for brightening up the outside of a small house or flat. Hanging baskets suspended from strong brackets are ideal for enlivening a plain stretch of wall. For supporting several hanging baskets, you can also buy maypole-like structures with arms branching out of the top.

## Ringing the changes

Because containers are portable, you can switch them around whenever you fancy a change of scene rather like re-arranging the furniture in your house, though the larger, heavy containers will need to be moved using a trolley or when they are empty. You can use a succession of containers – or a succession of different plants in the same container – to provide something new to look at all year round. Spare plants in containers can be used to fill a gap where a plant has died or perhaps is not looking its best.

From the design point of view, an attractive container helps make the most of a special plant, and provides a good

*Terracotta is a very popular material for containers – and it need not be limited to conventional flower pots. Here, an old chimney pot (above) is the basis for a delightful display of red ivy-leaved geraniums (pelargoniums) and blue lobelia. This is an ideal choice of plants for a sunny spot but always be sure to keep pots well watered in hot weather, up to twice a day in long hot spells.*

focal point in a corner, or at the end of a path. Containers also add character to a garden in their own right. You can choose ones that complement the style of your house – ultra-modern, traditional or cottagey. Or they can team with a particular style of planting: Mediterranean-look terracotta is ideal on a patio or for planting sub-tropical plants and herbs; stone is excellent for showing off alpines and rock plants; rustic wood is useful for shrubs like camellias. Containers come in a huge range of materials, shapes and sizes. You will probably keep the same ones for many years, so it pays to think carefully about which ones to buy.

### Low-cost containers

Plastic containers are the cheapest, but they tend to be short-lived. The cheaper plastics become brittle in sunlight, and crack after a few years out in the garden. They may even fall to bits completely when you try to move them, so take care if you move this kind when there are plants growing in them. Some plastic containers are designed only for use indoors or in a conservatory, so check the label or ask when you buy if you are not

*When it comes to choosing containers for your garden, you can really let your imagination run riot! In this case, an old mangle (right) has been painted bright red and filled with colourful bedding plants.*

*An old wheelbarrow that has outlived its usefulness need not be thrown away. With a simple coat of paint, it can be given a new lease of life as an unusual plant holder. This white-painted wheelbarrow (below) is host to a cheerful display of geraniums and petunias.*

Ann Kelly/Garden Picture Library

Eric Crichton

sure. If you are on a tight budget, plastic flower pots are the cheapest of all containers. Large sizes can double as tubs, and you could always tuck in a few trailing plants around the edge to hide the plastic.

### Traditional terracotta

Terracotta containers are popular. Clay flower pots are available in various sizes, often with optional saucers. They cost more than plastic pots do, but they are still a lot cheaper than many other types of container. You can also find decorative terracotta urns with raised patterns, and strawberry pots with planting pockets in the sides. When buying terracotta containers,

*Plant containers should harmonize with the style of your garden. Here, the classic formality of a Versailles tub (above) perfectly complements the modern simplicity of this seating area. The white-painted slats match those on the seat surround.*

### PLANT RELAY

Plunge pots of short-lived flowers like spring bulbs and some annuals up to their rims into a larger container filled with gravel. Then you can lift out and replace plants when they finish flowering without disturbing the display.

look for a label stating whether they are frost-proof or not. Pots that are not frost-proof, especially those with a neck, may crack if they are left out in the garden full of compost during winter – the water in the compost expands when it freezes and splits the pot. All is not totally lost if this happens, however, since the cracks can be repaired using

*This simple, stylish container (left) would look good in any modern setting. The understated look is emphasized by a cream and white colour scheme made up of nicotiana surrounded by a mass of white begonias.*

special adhesives (from DIY or craft stores). Broken terracotta pots also look good laid on their sides by a gravel path and used for growing sedums or sempervivums.

### Rustic look

Wooden tubs, half barrels and troughs are delightfully rustic. All wooden containers are liable to rot after a time, so treat them with wood preservative (choose one that is not poisonous to plants) and line the inside of the container with heavy-duty polythene before filling with compost.

Stone containers are expensive. Old stone sinks, carved from a whole chunk of rock, are now almost collectors' items, as are stone animal feeding troughs. Even so, many alpine enthusiasts like to get the real thing to show off their treasures to perfection. Synthetic stone, or reconstituted stone, is ground-up stone that has been moulded into the required shape.

Recycled and homemade containers are another option. Old chimney pots can still sometimes be bought from those builders' merchants who sell reclaimed old materials (look in your local directory, or ask a DIY shop or builder). Stood on end and filled with compost, they make lovely containers. For a similar, cheaper, effect you can use modern clay land drains.

### Clever fake

A discarded modern sink can be transformed into a fake stone one by plastering it outside with 'hypertufa' – a mixture of peat, gritty sand and cement that weathers to a rough stony finish. First clean the sink well inside and out. When it is dry, coat the outside with a layer of outdoor adhesive to provide a 'key' – as hypertufa will not stick to a smooth surface. Then mix equal parts of each ingredient in a bucket with enough water to make it just sloppy, and

Eric Crichton

*Plastic pots in shapes and designs similar to old metal ones can be 'antiqued' to give a similar look to the real thing (left). Just paint a dark grey paint over a dry lighter grey, and rub away part of the top coat while still wet to give 'highlights'.*

*For real budget gardening, empty paint pots can be turned into very effective containers (below). Remember to clean out the insides thoroughly first, and to drill drainage holes in the bottom.*

boxes to make a mould for a sink-shaped container. Choose two boxes that fit one inside the other, leaving a 2.5cm/1in gap all round. Spread a 2.5cm/1in-thick layer of hypertufa over the inside base of the larger box, then stand the smaller box inside. Trowel the remaining mixture into the gap between the two, and firm it gently down so there are no air pockets. Leave the hypertufa for several weeks before attempting to remove the cardboard boxes as it will take a long time to dry.

To prepare a container for planting, first clean it inside

paste it over the outside of the sink. If you want a really rough texture, use moss peat (also known as sphagnum peat or bog peat) instead of the cheaper sedge type. Allow several weeks for the 'stone' to set really hard. Once it is firm to touch, you can artificially 'age' it by painting it with natural yoghurt, or spraying it every few weeks with diluted liquid plant feed. Attractive outcrops of lichens and mosses will soon start to grow.

### Recycling

The same fake stone 'recipe' can also be used to coat other containers such as clay flower pots. You can even use it to make containers. One way is to fashion the basic shape from scrunched-up chicken wire (fine mesh metal garden netting), and coat it with a stiff hypertufa mixture. Alternatively, use two cardboard

Peter McHoy

(to remove any disease organisms left by previous plants) and outside (for appearance). Check there is at least one, and preferably several, drainage holes in the base. These are essential to allow excess water to run away.

### Winter care

Good drainage is vital for containers that will remain outside with plants in them over winter – waterlogged roots quickly rot and cause plants to die. If holes are needed in wood or metal, you can make them with an electric drill and the relevant bit. Holes can be made in plastic by heating up the tip of a skewer with a lighter or over a gas ring and pressing it through the base of the pot.

The next job is 'crocking'. Containers that have big drainage holes in the bottom should have large pieces of broken clay flower pot (crocks) placed over the holes to stop the compost clogging them up. Place crocks curved side down,

so water can run out but the compost cannot. Plastic pots with small drainage holes do not need crocking. Some plants, like alpines, need especially well-drained growing conditions – pour a 5cm/2in layer of gravel over the crocks before filling the container with compost.

### The right compost

The compost you use depends on the kind of plants you will be growing. For annuals, peat-based composts are ideal. If you are planting bulbs, or shrubs that will remain in the containers for several years on end, a soil-based John Innes compost is best. John Innes No. 3 (often called JI3) contains more plant food than JI1 or 2 and is best for established plants. Young plants should be planted in JI1. In either case, mix 10 per cent gritty sand or fine gravel with the compost to help drainage and provide weight (this helps keep the pots upright in windy weather). If you are growing lime-hating or acid-loving plants such as camellias, use a special ericaceous compost, again mixed with 10 per cent grit. And for growing alpines, which need well-drained but

moisture-retentive compost, make up your own mixture of one third each of JI3, gritty sand and coir fibre (also called coco peat).

If you are planting a single specimen in a container, simply treat it as if you were repotting a houseplant. Partly fill the container with loose compost. Knock the plant carefully out of its pot, tease out a few of the larger roots from the base of the rootball, stand it in the pot leaving 15mm/½in between the top of the rootball and the top of the pot, and refill around the roots with compost. Gently firm down the compost and water well.

### Group arrangement

If planting a group of different plants together in a large container, first arrange them *outside* the container. Do not plant them until you have the best possible combination of shapes, sizes and colours. Then plant as above.

Once planted up, containers do not require complicated care although they do need regular checking. Look at them daily and remove dead or dying flowers, then poke a finger into the compost and water it if it feels dry. Feed the plant

Roger Hyam/Garden Picture Library

*Whatever shape it comes in, the traditional terracotta pot (above) is always pleasing to the eye. Check before you buy, though, as some terracotta pots are not frost-proof and may crack in severe weather.*

Harry Smith

*Junk shops and market stalls can yield interesting finds for your garden, such as old washtubs or buckets. This unusual container (left) has been filled with a spring display of tulips and hyacinths.*

summer- and autumn-flowering kinds – are usually treated as temporary residents and dug up after flowering when the foliage dies down, then stored somewhere cool, dark and dry to replant again later.

### Out in the cold

Nowadays, though, people are increasingly interested in plants that can be put in containers and left out all year round. Evergreen shrubs and bamboos are useful here, but 'special' deciduous shrubs – especially the more compact kinds and small trees – also make good specimens for large pots. The pot tends to restrict the size of the plant, keeping it naturally dwarf.

Fruit trees such as patio peaches (a special dwarf kind), figs, a standard trained grape vine, or apples and pears grown on dwarfing rootstocks also make interesting container specimens, as do fruit bushes such as redcurrants. Or, for a strawberry pot, as an alternative to strawberries, try a collection of herbs, or several dwarf bush tomato plants like 'Totem'. And if you have space in a sunroom, greenhouse or conservatory in winter, why not try the new tender exotic shrubs and climbers. Compact plants like hardy ferns and many flowering perennials also make good permanent container plants.

Pat Brindley

### Miniature garden

Finally if you want something special to enjoy in close detail, rock plants are interesting, with perhaps a dwarf conifer for contrast. With a few extras like granite chippings spread over the compost between the different plants and the odd architectural chunk of rock, you can create a perfect garden in miniature.

*A blue-glazed Chinese pot (above) makes a very handsome holder for pink petunias and white alyssum. Containers like this are expensive, but you may find a similar but cheaper alternative in a second-hand shop. Most of these pots are not frost-proof.*

*This log container (below) is a perfect partner for the rustic wooden fence and stone wall in the background.*

regularly between spring and late summer with liquid or soluble plant feeds, following the manufacturer's instructions. Do not feed in winter. If tall plants need supports, push a few 45cm/18in green split canes in among them, and criss-cross between them with green garden twine.

### Suitable plants

The range of plants that can be grown in containers is tremendous. Annuals are always popular. But as well as the well-known summer annuals, do not forget small, early flowering plants like polyanthus, and for autumn and winter, favourites like winter-flowering pansies and ivy. Bulbs – of which you can find spring-,

Harry Smith

# Miniature Water Gardens

**Still waters need not necessarily run deep. You can create a miniature water garden in a pot or a tub and bring a tranquil beauty to your garden.**

*A half-barrel pond can stand proud, be sunk in a bed or half-sunk (above). This method gives some protection against cold weather, and stops the water being fouled by earth and gravel washed in by the rain.*

A tub or a half barrel can be transformed into a stunning, miniature water garden with remarkable ease, enabling you to enter the exciting and beautiful world of aquatic garden plants.

If your garden is very tiny you may have given up all thoughts of a water feature. A miniature pond in a container will solve this problem, provided you modify your ideas a bit. A wooden half barrel makes an excellent little pond, capable of sustaining a delightful, but necessarily small selection of water-loving plants.

There are lots of reasons for making a miniature water feature besides lack of space.

If you already have a full-sized pond in your garden, you may want to create another,

Andrew Lawson

Marijke Heuff/Garden Picture Library

## BRIGHT IDEAS

### POSSIBLE PLANTS

Marsh marigold or king cup (*Caltha palustris*) is a marginal plant that has lovely yellow flowers. It comes in single or double forms.

Monkey musk (*Mimulus luteus*) has varieties with yellow, orange or red spotted flowers. It is a marginal that needs to be kept under control.

*Scirpus zebrinus* is a marginal sedge that will give welcome vertical lines to your design. It is not as vigorous as other sedges, a positive advantage in this case.

*Calla palustris* is a bog arum with handsome foliage that will bring elegance to your pond. It is a tender marginal, so bring it in for winter or replace plants every year.

Planning a miniature pond is merely a matter of getting things into perspective. A container pond is not going to sustain a lot of plants and shoals of interesting, colourful fish.

### Being realistic

A dish in the middle of a table will take just one tiny water lily such as *Nymphaea pyg-*

smaller one to show off more delicate, specimen plants in a formal setting. Or you may use it like a garden nursery bed, to bring on plants eventually destined for the large pond.

### Creative containers

Patios and conservatories lend themselves to creative container gardening and a small pond can provide a delightful formal or informal focal point to such a display.

A miniature pond can be incorporated into your beds and borders as an attraction to frogs, toads and other wildlife. It will need to be sunk into the ground so that these delightful creatures can get in and out.

*The king cup* Caltha palustris *is a member of the buttercup family (top). Fully hardy, it bears bold clusters of golden flowers in the spring.*

*An unusual but effective option is to devote an area to several container ponds set at different heights (above). Here, one container grows a tall flowering rush, another a selection of low-growing bog plants, while the third provides a whimsical haven for a decoy duck.*

*A stone trough (right) also makes a pleasing miniature pond, especially when set in a courtyard garden.*

Ron Sutherland/Garden Picture Library

*maea* 'Alba', for example, and that is all. The simple elegance of such an arrangement will more than compensate for the lack of variety.

It is not a good idea to try to keep fish in a container pond, even one as large as a half barrel. Very tiny fish may cope with a miniature pond but they will soon be lost among the growing plants and you will rarely see them.

Most fish need a large surface area to their living quarters and a fair depth of water so that they do not get frozen solid in winter.

### Waterproofing
Wooden half barrels are an excellent choice and so are plastic tubs. Whatever you decide upon, the container must be scrubbed and rinsed thoroughly before you begin planting. If you select a half barrel, waterproofing may also be necessary.

Try filling the barrel with water first to see if the wood swells enough to stop seepage. Leave it for a reasonable length of time and top it up if need be. If the barrel still

Harry Smith Collection

leaks after this trial period you will need to waterproof it.

Use a proprietary waterproofing agent bought from a water garden centre or the bitumen paint commonly used for roofing purposes. Use caulking or sealer to fill odd cracks and holes.

Allow the waterproofing coat to dry out completely then fill the pond and leave it for a few days. Drain and refill the barrel several times before you plant to ensure that noxious residues are washed away.

### Sinking your pond
Your tub pond can be raised or sunken. If you decide to leave your tub standing on a patio

you will save yourself a lot of hard digging. However, there is more risk of damaging your plants because it may get frozen solid in winter.

If you choose this option, then place your plants in smaller, water-filled containers and bring them indoors at the end of the season.

Water lily and wildlife ponds must be sunken. Water lilies will not tolerate being frozen solid and there is less likelihood of this if you sink your tub in the ground.

Simply dig a hole a bit wider and deeper than your tub. Cover the bottom of your hole with compacted sand and work the base of the tub into

*An old sink (above) can provide a home for water plants. Lichens will grown on natural stone containers in shady spots.*

*A barrel must be planted selectively to avoid over-crowding. A water-lily with three or four foliage plants is the maximum (right).*

*The sedge Scirpus zebrinus (below) earns a place in a water garden with its unusual, horizontally-striped variegation.*

Pat Brindley

*The perfect blooms of Nymphaea pygmaea 'Alba' (right), about 2.5cm/1in across, put it in perfect scale with a miniature water garden.*

Andrew Lawson

## A LILY COLLECTION

Water lilies are the great favourites among aquatic plants. You could use a series of miniature ponds to form a small collection of these lovely surface plants.

Allow one container for each variety and make sure you site them where they will receive at least six hours sun a day. Remember that permanent lily ponds must be sunken to avoid being frozen solid.

There are several varieties particularly suitable for miniature water gardens:

*Nymphaea candida* is white and free blooming.

*N. tetragona* has pure white blooms.

*N. pygmaea* 'Alba' is also white. It will thrive in as little as 10-25cm/4-10in of water, making it and its other *pygmaea* cousins suitable for dishes and other small containers.

*N. pygmaea* 'Helvola' has dainty little yellow flowers and foliage mottled with burgundy.

*N. pygmaea* 'Rubra' has red flowers.

*N.* × *laydekeri* 'Purpurata' has wine red flowers and its relative *N.* × *laydekeri* 'Lilacea' is a softer shade of rose.

it. Use a spirit level to ensure that the tub is level. Fill the gaps at the side with compacted sand so that the tub is held firmly in place.

In time, the metal bands of the tub will rot away but the compacted sand will keep the tub securely in place.

### Planting

Care must be taken when planting a miniature water garden. You will ruin the look of your pond by stuffing it so full that you are left with a mass of dense vegetation and no clear water. This is not only unattractive to look at, but also bad for your plants.

It is far better to select just a few choice specimens. A water lily and two other suitable plants will look good together. Alternatively, just one water lily in glorious isolation can be

Peter McHoy

very elegant and all the more eye-catching because it is on its own.

Caution is necessary when choosing varieties as quite a number of water plants are on the vigorous side.

Fairy moss (*Azolla caroliniana*) and duckweed (*Lemna* spp.) are very invasive and will need netting out almost daily in midsummer. Once established, they are very difficult to eradicate.

### Irises

Irises, although a possibility, are difficult to integrate into a tub. They, too, can be invasive, but the main problem is that they may grow too tall and upset the balance of your design.

They tend to like very shallow water, which means raising planting baskets on bricks, taking up valuable room. If you feel you really must have an iris, choose very carefully.

As with garden plants, some aquatics are hardy and some will need protection from harsh weather. If you wish to grow a tender specimen in your tub you must overwinter the plant indoors.

*Just about any reasonably-sized, waterproof plant container can be pressed into service as a pond (above). Here, a plastic shrub tub is home to a dwarf water lily (Nymphaea pygmaea 'Helvola'), water plantain (Alisma plantago), with its spear-like leaves, an unusual form of water mint, Preslia cervina, and the floating fairy moss (Azolla caroliniana).*

*One of the most cheerily colourful of all the marginal plants is monkey musk (Mimulus luteus), whose yellow flowers (right) are randomly spotted and blotched with orange and red.*

# Pretty Pansies

**Pansies' velvety textures and friendly little faces make them one of the best-loved garden flowers, providing colour all year round.**

Derek Gould

**P**erhaps the pansy's place in our affections comes from its long association with lovers. The word pansy comes from the French *pensées,* meaning 'thoughts'. The charming flowers both of pansies and of their close relatives, violas, were said to turn a person's thoughts to their loved one. Their old English name, heartsease, symbolized the peace and rest that came to the hearts of lovers who died of love.

Yet, in stark contrast to this romantically melancholy image of tormented sweethearts, the pansy itself is essentially a cheerful plant. Not only does it present a bright and breezy countenance to the world, but it is amenable and obliging by nature too.

Pansies are simple to grow from seed and will put up with almost any soil. They are also very easy to obtain as bedding plants. Garden centres always carry a thorough selection and

most little local stores such as greengrocers, florists and even pet shops often offer trays of pansies for sale.

There are a host of varieties available, in almost every colour. Most varieties have at least two contrasting shades. In some cases this is a fringe around the petals; others have 'faces' of another colour at their centres.

If you browse through catalogues or the seed racks at your local garden centre, you

*The rich and varied colours of pansies (above) allow you to create an air of profusion in a small space and for little cost or effort. Some of the tones are unique and magical and, with care and a little luck, you can produce fine blooms throughout the year.*

will discover varieties of pansies for every season and, with care and a mild winter, you could have a colourful display all year round.

### Winter pansies

Winter can be a very dull time in your garden. This is especially true if your space is limited to a small patch, a balcony or a window box or two. There is simply no room for the shrubs, trees and heathers that provide most of the winter interest in larger gardens.

The ever-obliging pansy can brighten up the winter gloom. 'Winter Smiles' and 'Forerunner Mixed' are two colourful varieties which will flower from autumn through to early spring in mild winters.

The 'Universal' F1 hybrid varieties are also winter flowering and come in selections of

*You can really let your creativity show when you put pansies in hanging baskets. This ball-like effect (right) has a simple colour scheme. Just think what you can do with a richer mix! Pansies are hardy plants so your hanging basket can endure harsh days.*

*'King of the Blacks' (below) are among the most mysterious of all garden pansies. They are robust plants with flowers nestling deep in the foliage. They reach a breadth of 10cm/4in or more.*

Collections/Patrick Johns

## PLANT PROFILE

**Suitable site and soil:** will tolerate most soils but benefit from some prior preparation. Dig well and add well-rotted manure and a dusting of bone meal to the top 23cm/9in.

**Planting:** in spring or autumn, about 20-30cm/8-12in apart in full sun or partial shade.

**Propagation:** from seed or cuttings. Sow seeds according to the instructions on the packet. May be sown indoors or out. Cuttings should be taken from fresh new growth in spring or autumn. Stop the parent plant from flowering in July by removing buds, encouraging the vigorous new growth you will need in autumn. Choose sturdy stems and cut just below a joint. Trim away lower leaves. Add horticultural sand and perlite to the compost and fill trays to 10cm/4in. Make holes and add a little sand to the bottom of each. Firm in 6-8cm/2½-3in

cuttings and water well. Place in a shady spot. Plant out spring cuttings in autumn but over-winter autumn cuttings in a sunny, unheated cold frame.

**Pests and diseases:** rarely troubled by common pests such as slugs, snails and aphids. Red spider mite can sometimes be controlled by directing a jet of water at the creatures and their webs until all trace is washed away. The rare, soil-borne *pansy sickness* can kill off healthy plants almost overnight. Discard infected plants and start again in another site, or replace the topsoil in the infected area. Sinking pansies in pots into the bed is another solution.

**Recommended varieties:** Any 'Universal' will give winter flowers. Try 'Padparadja' and 'Clear Crystals' for self-colour and, for fun, 'Jolly Joker', the dwarf 'Baby Lucia' or 'Rippling Waters'.

Pat Brindley

Looking like a butterfly, the 'Joker Light Blue' pansy (left) has sharp colours and commands attention anywhere. The Joker varieties are among the ever-growing number of novelty plants whose patterns can be blended endlessly.

'Padparadja' (below) is named after a real jewel of the Orient. This plant takes on even more luxurious tones when planted among other pansies. A summer pansy, it offers a garden a broad swathe of colour or a rich splash in a drab corner.

### DEAD-HEADING

Remove the dead flowers from your pansies regularly so that they do not go to seed. Diligent dead-heading ensures that your plants continue to produce masses of flowers over a long period.

and summer varieties, plant some earlies. 'Eclipse' is one such variety, beginning its flowering very early in the season and finishing at the end of the summer. Another possible choice is 'Supremo', which offers yellow, bronze, red, rose, purple and white in its colour combinations. It has very large flowers.

'Ruffled Earlies', as their name suggests, have ruffled edges and flower in early spring. To add to their charms, they may sometimes have contrasting borders, veins, stripes or blotches.

### Summer blooms

Most pansies flower in summer and early autumn and there are many varieties to choose from in this category. Some of these can produce very large flowers, bi-coloured, tri-coloured or multi-coloured. 'Majestic Giant', 'Swiss Giant' and 'Monarch Giant' are all mixtures and will provide rich colours. Some of the blooms in these mixtures will have strongly marked faces.

For self-coloured pansies with a wide selection of colours, it is hard to beat the 'Clear Crystal Mixed' variety.

### Fancies

Among the summer lovers there is a wide choice of what Victorian gardeners referred to as 'fancies'. These are strikingly-coloured novelty plants whose numbers are added to every year. 'Jolly Joker', for instance, is an orange and purple bi-colour with a fairly small flower. 'Rippling Waters'

colours and types. The multi-coloured 'Delft', for example, has flowers that are lemon, cream, purple, white and midnight black, while 'Beaconsfield' is a beautiful royal purple shading to lilac, with light blue upper petals.

The unromantic sounding 'White Blotch' is a neat, compact plant, pure white with a deep violet blue face or 'blotch'. There is also a 'Blue Blotch', whose petals are a deep, rich blue tinged with purple. It has a distinctive velvet blue face.

If you prefer flowers in all one colour, without a face, the self-coloured varieties are for you. Amongst the winter flowerers there is 'True Blue', which is a clear mid-blue and has rather fetching whiskers. Other single-coloured varieties include a pure white and a wonderful apricot.

For smaller winter flowering plants choose 'Floral Dance', which will give you a lovely mixture of blooms. To ensure that there is no gap in flowering between the winter

is a splendid dark purple bloom enhanced with rippled white edges.

'Joker' is pale blue with a dark blue face and a little white for contrast. 'Love Duet' is cream suffused with pale pink and has a rich rose face.

For intensity of colour and a stunning display you could not do better than to choose 'Padparadja', which is a really deep, rich orange variety. It glows like the Sri Lankan jewel after which it is named. If you enjoy a really dramatic effect, plant it with the equally exotic 'Midnight Black' or another variety of the same colour, 'Black Star'.

## Choosing

Pansies offer such a wealth of possibilities in terms of colour, design and flowering season, that it is easy to get confused.

The first thing to decide is when you want them to flower. With care you can select varieties which will flower one after another so that every month of the year is graced by their presence in your garden.

The next consideration is where you want to plant them. Pansies are equally happy as border plants or container dwellers. They also make very effective edging plants.

Like most bedding plants, pansies enjoy full sun, but they will tolerate some shade.

Harry Smith Collection

S & O Mathews

This array of 'Monarch' pansies (left) have been orchestrated to resemble a painting. 'True Blue' pansies (below left) are a reminder that they can be subtly shaded as well as vibrantly coloured.

The aptly named 'Jolly Joker' (above) is among the most reliable pansies for summer blooms.

The exquisite 'Love Duet' (right) is one of the most striking of all pansy varieties.

Derek Gould

## PERFECT PARTNERS

Harry Smith Collection

Potted pansies look good when combined with slightly taller flowers. These blue violas and white tulips (above) make a dramatic effect.

Unlike their close relatives, violets and some violas, they are not suited to brightening a very shady corner.

### Mix and match

Design is the next consideration. Many devotees of the pansy feel that they are at their resplendent best when masses of the same variety are planted together in a border or container. This is particularly true of self-coloured varieties.

However, pansies also make good companion plants. The more old-fashioned varieties, for example, make a handsome addition to a knot garden. Their old-world charm blends beautifully with the historical theme of this type of planting scheme. Box hedges and the foliage of selected herbs make a wonderful background for their jaunty, colourful blooms. Choose fairly tidy herbs such as chives, thyme, parsley and basil. Pansies cannot compete with unruly types such as mint.

Pansies look well with small bulbs such as snowdrops, *Iris reticulata*, cyclamen and muscari. Their bold colours and markings complement the more delicate features of miniature bulbs. The shapes go well together too.

# Busy Lizzies

**If you are looking for an easy, reliable annual to add colour to your garden throughout the summer, then the aptly-named busy Lizzie is the plant for you.**

Everything about busy Lizzies suggests bright, cheerful bustle. This bushy, succulent-stemmed and almost perpetual-flowering plant was given its common name because of its fast growth and the persistence with which it flowers. Seedlings begin to produce blooms when they are only an inch or so tall, and carry on doing so all through the summer months.

Even its generic name, *Impatiens*, suggests swift movement, though in this case it is named not for its growth habits but rather for the speed with which it discharges its seeds when ripe.

*Busy Lizzies are enormously versatile plants. Several different varieties planted together in a bed make a colourful ground cover (right), while a single variety will grace a tub or window-box (below). If they are left in their pots, other options arise. Wedging the pots in the gaps in a honeycomb wall, for example, enables the plants to make lovely vertical cover (opposite above).*

*A striking alternative to conventional busy Lizzies is provided by the new, larger-flowered New Guinea hybrids, some with variegated foliage (opposite below).*

Peter McHoy

Derek Gould

Peter McHoy

a pronounced spur at the back.

None of the new compact strains is likely to grow beyond a height of 30-40cm/12-15in, which makes them ideal candidates for hanging baskets, small tubs and window boxes, though they are equally good performers when planted out as summer bedding. They are extremely versatile and can safely be used in difficult, shady parts of the garden or in full sunshine: not many half-hardy annuals tolerate both conditions. There will, naturally, be more flowers if the plant is grown in full sun.

Among the many hybrid strains of *Impatiens* are plants with flowers of all shades of

The ancestral strains of *Impatiens* originated in the tropical and sub-tropical areas of Africa and the Far East.

From these tall, rangy ancestors have been developed a vast range of hybrids that have all of the good habits and none of the drawbacks of the parent plant. Most busy Lizzie hybrids are notable for their compact, low-growing habit and for their profuse blooming. The flowers are generally single, though there are some spectacular doubles, and have

John Glover/Garden Picture Library

## PLANT PROFILE

**Suitable site and soil** Does well in full sun or partial shade. Will tolerate most soil conditions if kept moist, but not waterlogged.

**Planting** Plant out young specimens when all danger of frost has passed. Prepare the border by working in a little well-rotted garden compost and sprinkle in a handful of bone meal to enrich the area around the roots of each plant; they should be placed 15-23cm/6-9in apart. Water in.

**Cultivation and care** Require little attention apart from regular watering when the rain does not oblige.

**Propagation** If growing from seed, this should be sown indoors or under glass in spring. Use peat-based compost and cover the seeds lightly. Seedlings must be kept at a temperature of at least 18°C/65°.

When they are about 4cm/1½in high, transplant them into individual pots of loam-based compost. Alternatively, tip cuttings 5-8cm/2-3in long can be taken in summer or early autumn and rooted in water before being potted up.

**Pests and diseases** Slugs can be a problem to younger, weaker plants and aphids may occasionally take a fancy to the odd specimen.

**Recommended varieties** So many varieties have been developed that it is difficult to make a choice. Here are some to look out for.

● The fast-growing 'Imp' and 'Super Elfin' strains grown to around 23cm/9in high and produce large flowers in a full range of colours.

● 'Novette' mixture, with plants only 10cm/4in high, and 'Florette' (15cm/6in) are good for edging and for the front of mixed borders.

● 'Futura', which has a trailing habit, is ideal for window boxes and hanging baskets.

● 'Camellia flowered Mixed' (45cm/18in) and 'Tom Thumb Mixed' (20cm/10in) are best for the balsam-type double flowers; 'Confection Mixed' is the choice for conventional doubles.

● 'Zig-Zag', which has striped blooms, is extremely eye-catching, while 'Grand Prix' bears the largest flowers.

Harry Smith Collection

Eric Crichton

pink, red, orange, mauve and white. There are also bi-coloured varieties – for instance, red or pink striped with white.

The leaves may be elliptic or heart-shaped and can be coloured in almost every imaginable shade of green; some have a bronze or purple sheen and reddish or brown speckles on the undersides.

### Named varieties

Although they are raised from named types, in garden centres you may be faced with rows of plants marked simply 'Impatiens F1 Hybrid', giving the colour and brief information on the height, spread and general care of the plant.

However, if you wish to look further into the various varieties, a specialist grower should be able to identify and supply a much wider range of named

Impatiens hybrids.

The best way to get a named variety, though, is to raise plants from seed. As a basic bedding plant for borders and large containers, it is difficult to beat the fast-growing 'Imp' and 'Super Elfin' varieties. Both grow to around 23cm/9in tall and produce large flowers in a full range of colours.

If you have smaller containers, try the dwarf 'Novette' mixture. This free-flowering variety grows to just 10cm/4in tall, making it a good choice for edging a border. The same is true of the slightly taller (15cm/6in) 'Florette' series.

The compact colour they provide make busy Lizzies a good choice for window boxes; the semi-pendulous habit of the 'Futura' variety makes it ideal for boxes and for hanging baskets, where it makes a good companion for trailing

Harry Smith Collection

*Photo credit: Pat Brindley*

*Photo credit: Peter McHoy*

*Named varieties are not always available as bedding plants, but they can be raised from seed without much difficulty, and are well worth the effort. The striped blooms of 'Zig Zag' (left) make a striking display for a container or hanging basket, while the small blooms of the dwarf form, 'Novette Mixed' (below left) make excellent bedding plants for the front of a border. 'Super Elfin Mixed' (right) is a taller variety, with correspondingly larger flowers. Large flowers are also characteristic of the New Guinea hybrids; the pink and white blooms of 'Fanfare' (below right) are set off by handsomely variegated leaves. Impatiens F1 hybrids include several double-flowered varieties. Although some are named, others are simply sold as 'Double Mixed' (below). Sometimes the double flowers resemble roses; others are more open.*

## GARDEN NOTES

### HARDENING OFF

It is essential that you wait until the possibility of frost is past and the soil is beginning to warm up before planting out. This means the beginning of summer at the earliest.

Accustom the plants to outside conditions by introducing the pots to the garden for lengthening periods, making sure that you bring them in at night. Do not allow them to dry out during this hardening-off period – this can happen very quickly to plants in small pots – but be very careful not to over-water either, as the plants will rot in water-logged soil.

---

pelargoniums, fuchsias, petunias and lobelia.

Complex double varieties, no less free-flowering, are available for those who want to put on a little more show in their borders.

The camellia-flowered busy Lizzies (which are usually called balsam, the name under which you will find them in some catalogues) are varieties

### NEW BLOOMS

Striking new hybrids with larger flowers have recently been developed as a result of a plant-gathering expedition to New Guinea. Some strains reputedly produce flowers over 8cm/3in across. Many of the most colourful have strongly variegated foliage.

These New Guinea hybrids are now becoming available through garden centres and mail-order catalogues.

of *I. balsamina*, and come in shades of rose, blush pink, scarlet and white. 'Camellia Flowered Mixed', one of the largest busy Lizzie varieties, grows to 45cm/18in. The same type of showy flower can be had in smaller plants; try 'Tom Thumb Mixed' (25cm/10in).

There are double-flowered forms of the more conventional busy Lizzie, too, such as 'Confection Mixed' (20-30cm/8-12in tall, with fine, double and semi-double flowers).

### Growing busy Lizzies

Strictly speaking, *Impatiens* is a perennial. Growers of houseplants will be well aware of the busy Lizzie's sterling service indoors – a well cared for specimen can be kept at peak performance for years.

However, when grown as a garden plant in temperate conditions it must be regarded

as a tender half-hardy annual. Most modern *Impatiens* hybrids are started off in spring under glass and discarded in the autumn before the first frosts puts paid to them. Young plants can be purchased through mail-order catalogues and begin to appear in garden centres in late spring.

They may, of course, be propagated from seed at home, though this will have to be done indoors, as seedlings must be kept at a minimum temperature of 18°C/65°F.

Seed should be sown on a growing medium based on peat or a peat substitute in spring and lightly covered. When the seedlings are large enough to handle (about 4cm/1½in tall), transplant them into individual pots of loam-based compost. Pinch out the growing tips of young plants regularly to ensure bushiness.

Alternatively, you can take tip cuttings 5-8cm/2-3in long from existing plants in the summer and root them in water. Transfer them to a soil-based compost when roots 1½cm/½in long have formed, and over-winter them indoors.

Whole plants can also be lifted from the garden and

*The camellia flowered busy Lizzies (above) are varieties of I. balsamina and are often sold as balsam. Unlike other Impatiens hybrids, they are true annuals. Most varieties have an upright growth habit, and do not branch. While the species has small, single flowers, hybrids are fully double; the flower stems are very short and the blooms appear to burst out from between the lance-shaped leaves.*

*Facing page: a colourful summer border filled with busy Lizzies. If carefully tended, busy Lizzies will last throughout the summer and into the autumn.*

## GROWING TIPS

### INDOOR PESTS

When you are raising plants indoors, they can be susceptible to pests which also enjoy the warm conditions. This is especially true if you have a large collection of houseplants.

Red spider mite can be a real menace if conditions become very dry, causing mottling and bronzing of leaves, which may begin to drop.

Whitefly is another nuisance. It disfigures and weakens the plants. In each case, treat with a suitable systemic insecticide such as dimethoate.

then over-wintered indoors. Usually, though, they have become so leggy by the end of the summer that they are not worth hanging on to.

### Planting out

Whichever method of propagation you choose, or whether you simply decide to start again with new plantlets each year, do take care not to plant them out too early. Always harden them off gradually, accustoming them to lower temperatures and more airy conditions for a week or two before planting them out in their final positions.

Once the danger of their main enemy, frost, is past, busy Lizzies could not be ea-

sier to grow. There are, however, always the usual garden pests around, ready to prey on vulnerable individuals.

Slugs and snails may attack seedlings and young plants, especially in periods of wet weather. A sprinkling of slug pellets from time to time should keep them at bay.

Also, keep an eye out for infestations of aphids on leaves or stems, which will weaken the plants, make them sticky and encourage mould.

Once summer is under way, all you really need to do is keep your plants well-watered, and they will reward you with a heartening display of colour throughout the season and well into the autumn.

# French and African Marigolds

**Bring touches of gold and bronze to every corner of your garden with these long-lasting, and trouble-free annuals.**

Pat Brindley

**W**ith their showy, long-lasting blooms, tidy growth habit and sturdy stems, French and African marigolds are among the most popular and easy-to-grow annuals in the yellow and orange colour range. They are equally happy in city, suburban and country gardens, and as attractive in formal bedding schemes as in informal mixed borders. They are also ideal for containers and window boxes.

In spite of their names, French and African marigolds are Mexican in origin, and are half-hardy annuals belonging to the daisy, or *Compositae*, family. They grow, according to the type and variety, from 13.5-90cm/5in-3ft high, and flower non-stop, from early summer until the first frost.

The flowers can be single and daisy-like, fully double like carnations, or have petals around a central crest. Bright yellow and orange are traditional colours, but there are vivid mahogany red and lemon yellow varieties too. Some varieties have two-toned flowers, with striped, edged or blotched petals. The dark-green, deeply divided, glossy leaves have a distinctive pungent scent when crushed.

African marigolds *(Tagetes erecta)* are also called Aztec or American marigolds. These are the real show-stoppers, with massive double yellow or orange blooms, 7.5cm-20cm/3-8in across, densely packed with petals. They have a stiff, upright habit, and are branching but not bushy.

Tall varieties, 60-90cm/2-3ft high, include 'Sovereign', with golden yellow flowers; 'Doubloon', with light yellow

Photos Horticultural

*The French marigold (Tagetes patula) is available in both single and double-flowered forms in either solid yellow, orange or mahogany red, or in interesting two-tone effects like this double variety 'Russet Sophia' (left) and single 'Susanna' (below).*

Harry Smith

64

## BRIGHT IDEAS

### PERFECT FOR DRYING

You can preserve the bright colour of African marigolds all year round by air drying them. Orange varieties are best. Pick when they are just fully open, on a dry, sunny day. Cut the stem short and insert a fine stub wire, available from florists, up the hollow stem and into the flower head. Bend at the top to secure, then hang in a dry, warm spot out of direct sunlight. As they dry, the flowers shrink, but the colour remains surprisingly clear.

flowers; 'Hawaii', rich orange; and 'Sierra Mixed', with light yellow, dark yellow and orange flowers. 'Giant Fluffy Mixed', ruffled and fully double, like huge chrysanthemums; and 'Toreador', with rich orange blooms, are also worth trying.

Dwarf varieties, 25-30cm/10-12in high, include 'Moonbeam', with very pretty pale yellow flowers. The compact, uniform, F1 hybrid 'Inca' series, available in mixed and single colours, includes 'Sunshine Mixed', 'Inca Orange' and 'Inca Gold'.

French marigolds (*T. patula*) grow 15-30cm/6-12in high, with either single, daisy-like

*French marigolds look particularly effective planted in drifts (above) rather than dotted about singly or in groups of two or three.*

*If you will be looking at your marigolds from a distance, single colours tend to be most effective. If, on the other hand, you can grow some in window boxes or other containers, you will be more able to appreciate subtle colour combinations like those of this French marigold 'Bolero' (above).*

*The dwarf 'Inca' series of African marigolds comes in mixed and single colours, including this striking 'Inca Gold' (left).*

## PLANT PROFILE

**Suitable site and soil:** ordinary, well-drained soil and sun are best, though fertile soil produces the biggest blooms. Dig over the soil before planting, remove all weeds and work in some well-rotted garden compost or sterilized organic compost, available in bags from garden centres.

**Planting:** plant out after the last frost, in late spring or early summer. A week before planting, put the trays or pots outside during the day, in a sunny, sheltered spot, to harden off the plants. (Bring them in again at night or in cold weather.)

Space dwarf varieties 20cm/8in apart, ordinary varieties 30cm/12in apart, and tall African marigolds 45cm/18in apart. Press down the soil or potting compost around the stem with your hand or the back of a trowel. Water in well.

**Cultivation and care:** continue watering until established, then only in long dry spells. Remove faded flowers to keep plants looking tidy and to encourage more flower buds to form. For extra large African marigold flowers, pinch off all but the top flower bud, as soon as the side buds appear. Tall varieties may need staking on exposed sites. Dig up and discard plants after the first autumn frost, since they will not bloom again.

**Propagation:** sow seed under glass in early or mid-spring, 6-8 weeks before the last expected spring frost. Cover the seeds lightly with seed compost. Keep at a steady temperature (18°C/64°F) and just moist; the seeds should sprout quickly. As soon as the seedlings are large enough to handle, gently transplant into trays, 5cm/2in apart in each direction, or into pots.

**Pests and diseases:** slugs and snails love marigolds, so use slug pellets. Botrytis, or grey mould, can attack plants in damp conditions, and can rot flower heads.

or double flowers, often with a densely packed central 'crest'. They can be in solid colours of yellow, orange or mahogany red, or striped, splashed, mottled, edged or tinged in a contrasting colour.

Attractive single varieties include 'Cinnebar', 30cm/12in high, which has burgundy-red flowers with yellow centres. The 25cm/10in high 'Naughty Marietta' has gold flowers with dark centres, while 'Sunny' is 30cm/12in high, with golden yellow, frilly flowers and 'Burgundy Ripple' is 30cm/12in high with rich, gold-edged orange-red flowers.

Double varieties of French marigold include the early-flowering 'Holiday Crested Mixed', 30cm/12in high, with large, uniform flowers, perfect for bedding or edging. 'Tiger Eyes', 30-35cm/12-14in high, has scarlet and dark orange chrysanthemum-like blooms, while 'Honeycomb', 25cm/10in high, has densely packed russet petals, edged in gold.

For window boxes, the 15cm/6in high 'Boy O' Boy' has bright orange flowers on compact plants. Unusually tolerant of wet or dry weather is 'Spanish Brocade', 20cm/8in high, with golden-edged, dark orange blooms. And for fully double, scarlet, camellia-like flowers, choose 'Scarlet Sophie', 25-30cm/10-12in high.

For a carpet effect grow 'Teeny Weeny'. Only 12cm/5in high, it forms a low-spreading mass of foliage, with single red and yellow blooms.

### Afro-French marigolds

Sometimes called mule marigolds because they are sterile and do not set seed, Afro-French marigolds are F1 Triploid hybrids. Most are 25-40cm/10-16in high, and 30cm/12in across. They combine the shorter, bushier habit of French marigolds with the enormous, double blooms of African marigolds.

Good .varieties include the bright-yellow 'Showboat', the

mahogany-tinged gold 'Seven Star Red' and the mixed 'Red and Gold Hybrids', up to 60cm/2ft high. 'First Lady' has clear yellow flowers, while 'Pineapple Crush', a dwarf form, 20cm/8in high, has buttercup-yellow blooms and the similar-sized 'Pumpkin Crush' has rich orange blooms.

### Plants and seeds

When buying trays or pots of young plants, choose leafy, compact plants with plenty of

*You can create different colour schemes with your marigolds, depending on the plants you choose to grow with them. This Tagetes tenuifolia 'Lemon Gem' looks 'warm' when it is growing next to the rich red and purple fuchsia, but much 'cooler' when it is combined with white alyssum.*

Harry Smith

Photos Horticultural

Harry Smith

WHAT WENT WRONG?

## UNSUCCESSFUL SEEDS

**Q** Last spring I bought a pack of Afro-French marigold seeds and followed the instructions carefully, but only twelve plants ever came up. What did I do wrong?

**A** Probably nothing. Although they are fabulous plants, their one drawback is a lower than average germination rate. This year, buy two packs, and you should end up with plenty for a good display. Remember, too, that Triploid hybrid seed packs often contain fewer seeds than other types – check the packet before you buy.

*Dwarf marigolds like these Tagetes tenuifolia (above) are useful for softening the edge of a path or lawn, but do not let this blind you to the glories of the taller varieties when viewed en masse, like this Tagetes tenuifolia 'Paprika Mixed' (below).*

GO ORGANIC!

## MARIGOLD WARFARE

African and French marigolds are traditional 'companion' plants, planted in rows in the vegetable garden. The strong scent of their leaves deters harmful insects from attacking crops. The roots of some species actually excrete a substance that can deter or even kill some soil pests.

flower buds. Avoid over-crowded plants and any with yellow leaves. Those in full flower may be tempting, but you will get a longer display if you stick to healthy plants in bud, with some colour showing, and maybe just one or two open blooms.

If you are buying seed packets, check the sell-by date. F1 hybrids have the largest, most uniformly sized and shaped flowers, especially important for formal bedding. They are more expensive than non-F1 hybrids, but you will find the difference in results well worth the extra initial cost.

### Colour and form

Solid-colour African and French marigolds tend to have more impact from a distance than multi-coloured varieties, especially if the colour pattern is lacy or complex. Bright colours, such as lemon yellow or sharp orange, stand out well, especially against dark foliage. If, on the other hand, you want a rich, subtle effect, go for darker tones, or multi-coloured varieties featuring dark tones.

For an informal or wild garden, small, single flowers on spreading, bushy plants are

best, since they can mingle to form a solid mass. For a formal scheme, on the other hand, double flowers and narrow, upright plants are ideal.

If you want a riot of colour, some varieties are so prolific that the flowers completely hide the foliage, but for a more natural look, choose one with a high proportion of foliage to the number of flowers.

### Display ideas

All French and African marigolds are ideal for container growing, since they have small root systems. Dwarf forms especially make first-class window box plants.

You can plant French and African marigolds in straight lines or blocks, or use them to edge a flower bed or path. Planted in groups of odd numbers, such as three, five, seven or nine, they can be used to create irregularly shaped clumps of colour.

Indoors, African and French marigolds are excellent as cut flowers, and both the whole flowers and the petals can be dried for flower arrangements, pressed flower pictures or for adding colour to pot pourri.

# Nostalgic Nasturtiums

**Nasturtiums are old favourites in cottage gardens. Although mostly used as bedding plants, they will also climb, trail or add spice to your salad.**

Photos Horticultural

Nasturtiums are homely plants that most people like to have around because they are cosy and familiar. Bright, cheerful and easy going, their very lack of temperament has meant they have attracted little in the way of keen interest from most competitive growers.

Fuchsias, delphiniums and others can become an obsession and have whole books dedicated to describing their likes and dislikes, but the obliging nasturtium usually warrants a mere few lines at best. However, there is far more interest to these humble charmers than this lack of attention would suggest.

### A place in history

Nasturtiums were well known in Elizabethan England. Their peppery leaves and attractive flowers were much prized as an ingredient of salads. In fact, the name 'Nasturtium' rightly belongs to that other peppery character, watercress. The confusion arose as the newcomer from the West Indies came to be known as 'Indian Cress.' The plant's correct botanical name is *Tropaeolum majus*.

Since their introduction hundreds of years ago, nasturtiums have maintained a steady popularity. No self-respecting cottage garden could do without their vibrant colours – shades of orange, red and yellow – and easy ways. In more modern times they have continued to prove their worth. They need very little attention, which is a real bonus for those busy people with little gardening time.

When people think of nasturtiums they are usually picturing that annual favourite, *Tropaeolum majus* or the garden nasturtium. However, there are several others in the same genus, coming in three main groups; climbers, trailers and bedding varieties. Their versatility makes them ready, willing and able to adapt to life in any kind of container, a useful trait, especially if you are short of space.

It is possible to grow some as perennials, while others are too tender to survive all but the mildest of winters. Some have the lush, vibrant good looks of jungle creepers while even the more familiar garden nasturtium has several exotic varieties, such as 'Alaska',

*Usually thought of as summer bedding plants, the ever obliging nasturtiums will fill all manner of unlikely nooks and crannies with warm, cheerful colour, whether the flowers are peeking out from beneath a hedge, clambering over a tree stump or cascading prettily in long trails down a wall or bank (above).*

There are many more colours than orange and yellow in the nasturtium's palette. 'Peach Melba' (left) is a variety of Tropaeolum majus *whose pale, creamy petals each have a blotch of orange at the base. In some varieties, extra colour is presented by the foliage; 'Alaska' (below) has leaves randomly splotched and veined with white and cream. Quite the most unusual colour in the genus, however, is provided by the heavenly blue notched petals of the rarely-grown climber* Tropaeolum azureum *(bottom).*

Pat Brindley

Andrew Lawson

Harry Smith Collection

## PLANT PROFILE

**Suitable site and soil** Most prefer a fair amount of sun, but will tolerate dappled shade. Annual nasturtiums positively prefer poor soil. All types require good drainage.

**Cultivation and care** Just make sure that the site has good drainage. Dig the site over and remove any annual or perennial weeds. Do not add any kind of feed as this will only serve to produce vigorous foliage at the expense of the flowers.

**Propagation** From seed, which may be planted in early spring where they are to flower. Alternatively, seed may be germinated in gentle heat early in the year and planted out in spring. Some varieties may be propagated from tubers or basal cuttings.

**Pests and diseases** Blackfly is the main villain. It tends to infest the underside of the leaves, especially where the leaf meets the stalk. Use a proprietary spray or regular douches of soft soap and water. A well-balanced organic garden may have enough predatory insects to cope with the problem.

Caterpillars of the cabbage white butterfly and its close relatives may be a pest. Spray with trichlorphon or dust with derris powder. Organic alternatives are to pick them off by hand or, if the infestation is fairly light, to simply sacrifice the odd plant for the pleasure of having butterflies in your garden.

with its splendid, marbled and blotched variegated foliage.

Several species are natural, born climbers. Perhaps the most unusual, in terms of colour, as well as one of the most difficult to find, is the herbaceous *Tropaeolum azureum*, which bears small, purple-blue flowers late in the summer. Although this plant is technically a perennial, it will not survive frost, so must be seen as an annual in areas where winter frosts are inevitable.

*T. peregrinum*, also known as *T. canariense*, is the well-known canary creeper –

Pat Brindley

Eric Crichton

Eric Crichton

named for its canary-yellow flowers rather than for any connection with the Canary Islands. This is another frost-tender plant that will only survive the winter in the mildest of climates. Its small, bright flowers are set off by grey-green leaves. It will grow to a height of 2m/6ft or more.

### Hardy climbers
A frost-hardy climber is the flame creeper (*T. speciosum*). This member of the nasturtium family has striking red flowers in the summer months, followed by rather handsome, bright blue fruits nestling among the deep red remnants of the outer parts of the flowers, the calyces.

This lovely plant enjoys having its head in full sun but its roots in shade. It climbs to a height of 3m/10ft and is useful for covering fences, walls or dead trees. It is herbaceous,

*Tropaeolum peregrinum, the canary creeper (above), is named for its delightful flowers, bright yellow with a feathery fringe. It is a tender perennial, but easily raised from seed and best treated as an annual. A vigorous climber, it will put on 2.4m/8ft of growth in a good season.*

dying back to take a well-earned rest in winter.

*T. tuberosum*, 'Ken Aslet' is another handsome member of the nasturtium group of plants, with small red and orange trumpet-shaped flowers flourishing from mid-summer to autumn. It grows from tubers, as it name suggests, so although it is not frost-hardy, its tubers may be dug up and stored for next year. It is a particularly useful plant in exposed or coastal areas, as it will cheerfully put up with

*The gorgeous colours of the single-flowered 'Whirlybird' series (top) have made this relatively new variety a great favourite among lovers of dwarf nasturtiums.*

*Many nasturtium varieties will happily climb or trail. This one's variegated leaves are set off to perfection if they are allowed to tumble lazily on to a paved patio (above).*

wind and salt sprays.

Several other varieties will climb, including *T. majus* 'Tall Mixed' and *T. peltophorum* 'Spitfire'. These two varieties look lovely cascading down dry banks or swarming over unsightly constructions.

### Trailers

This group is dominated by the *T. majus* 'Gleam' hybrids. The colours available include bright red, orange and yellow and may be bought as mixtures or in single colours.

These are the nasturtiums most suitable for use in hanging baskets or to trail over the front of window boxes and containers. Their bright colours and handsome leaves bring a cheerful, informal look to your garden or patio. They have double flowers and will grow to about 30-45cm/1-1½ft.

### Bedding plants

All nasturtiums suitable for bedding plants are varieties of *T. majus*. 'Empress of India' grows to a height of 20cm/8in

### NATURAL CONTROL

The natural way to control aphids, including blackfly, is to encourage a well-balanced community of insects. This means not using sprays.

Hoverfly larvae have a voracious appetite – each eats around 600 aphids. You can attract these welcome visitors with the right plants.

Adult hoverflies love plants that give easy access to their nectar. So plant bold displays of poached egg plant (*Limnanthes douglasii*), *Convolvulus tricolor* 'Blue Ensign' and pot marigold (*Calendula officinalis*) among nasturtiums to bring nature's own aphicide to your garden.

*GO ORGANIC!*

and is vigorous and bushy in habit. Its dark crimson flowers give a fine show between early summer and autumn.

The 'Jewel' series of nasturtiums are particularly useful

Harry Smith Collection

### SUMMER SHOW

Winter flowering shrubs can be dull in summer when all they have to show is their foliage.

Cheer them up by growing *T. peregrinum*, (Canary creeper) over them in the summer months. The lovely, bright yellow flowers will swarm all over the shrub, brightening it up with a much-needed splash of colour and blooms.

*BRIGHT IDEAS*

**Tropaeolum tuberosum** *(right) is a tender herbaceous climber whose tubers must be lifted and overwintered in a warm place if it is to survive the winter. However, it rewards the extra effort with handsome, trumpet-shaped, spurred, bi-coloured flowers that are produced in great profusion from the middle of summer through to the autumn.*

The 'Gleam' series of T. majus varieties have a trailing habit, making them the most popular choice for hanging baskets, window boxes or other raised containers. These double-flowered varieties, such as 'Golden Gleam' (right), are sold in the usual range of colours, either by the variety or in a mix.

Pat Brindley

# PERFECT PARTNERS

Derek Gould

The perennial flame creeper (*T. speciosum*) dies back in winter. Planting it with a variegated ivy (above) sustains interest and cover.

as bedding plants because their semi-double flowers are held in plain view above the leaves. This is not always the case, and in many varieties the flowers can be hidden by exuberant foliage.

Another compact dwarf variety is 'Whirlybird': once again the flowers are held proudly above the foliage. The 'Whirlybird' series can be bought in mixed or single colours; all have simple, single flowers.

'Peach Melba' is another popular variety; it has pale yellow flowers blotched with scarlet. Like 'Jewel' and 'Whirlybird', this variety grows to about 30cm/1ft.

## Simple needs

Most varieties of nasturtiums are really easy to please. The majority actually prefer poor soil, which means you are spared the trouble of preparing a special bed for them. All they require is a little elbow room and good drainage.

Propagation is simple, too. Annuals grow from seed, and basal cuttings can be taken from herbaceous varieties. Some grow from tubers and may be divided.

For *T. majus* varieties simply sow the seed in spring where the plants are to flower and keep the ground moist until the seedlings are established. If you want early colour, you can germinate your seeds in gentle heat during late winter and plant out when all threat of frost has passed.

Blackfly is the most likely pest; in fact, blackfly heaven is probably full of broad beans underplanted with nasturtiums. They can be controlled by spraying with an insecticide, but dousing them with soapy water is better – if a little less effective – if you want to encourage other, less destructive insects, like butterflies, into your garden.

# *Sumptuous Pelargoniums*

**A bright summer display of pelargoniums – often known as geraniums – will give your garden the Mediterranean touch.**

**P**elargoniums provide non-stop colour in sunny beds and borders as well as in containers, window boxes and hanging baskets. They provide bright flowers over a long period as well as attractively marked leaves to suit your seasonal colour schemes. Use them to create decorative features in every part of your garden this summer.

Pelargoniums come from hot, sunny climates, so give them the warmest position to make sure they thrive – though they will tolerate a little shade. They are tender and, if you wish to keep them growing from year to year, you will need to bring them indoors (or into a greenhouse) during the winter.

### Planting out

Start your plants off on their annual growing season indoors and, once the danger of frost is past, set them out into their flowering positions in sunny borders or garden containers. You can also grow pelargoniums from seed or from small plantlets sold by nurseries or specialised outlets.

The flowers, usually carried in quite densely packed mophead clusters, have five petals in the single varieties, and more in the double. Colours range from hot reds and oranges, through to deep burgundy and pale pinks. There are also white varieties. The soft leaves are sometimes

*Pelargoniums are perfect container plants. In this stone 'geranium pot' (right) red and pink flowers cascade to great effect.*

Neil Holmes

Gillian Beckett

Tania Midgley

*Pelargonium 'Apple Blossom' (above) is a zonal variety with particularly attractive double pink and white flowers. Other similar recommended varieties include 'Layton White' with its white single flowers and 'Penny', which has pretty pink double flowers.*

*Regal pelargoniums (below) are showy hybrids best on their own in pots so their colour and shape can be fully appreciated. There are a number of very beautiful varieties, including 'Grand Slam' with its bright red flowers and 'Autumn Festival' which has pink flowers with white throats.*

attractively marked or coloured. You can use these showy plants in blocks of a single colour, but by choosing more subtle colours and combining them with other harmonious plants, you can create an integrated and stylish effect.

Pelargoniums come in an amazing array of shapes and sizes. The four most popular groups that you will enjoy using in the garden are zonal, regal, ivy-leaved trailing and scented-leaf types.

## Popular pelargoniums

Zonal pelargoniums (*P. × hortorum*) offer a great variety of flower shapes and leaf colouring. There are single and double-flowered forms as well as some with spidery, cactus-like flowers and others with tightly rolled 'rosebud' flowers. The most common leaf colour is green, but the leaves usually have a horseshoe-shaped zone or dark line breaking up the solid green colour.

Golden to amber leaves, two-colour variegation (usually green and cream) and tri-coloured leaves are also possible. All these variations add to the overall versatility of pelargoniums. There are also miniature and dwarf forms.

Regal pelargoniums (*P. × domesticum*) are hybrids bred from several different species and, although they are often used as houseplants, they can also be used in outdoor containers in the summer. They have large flowers (up to 5cm/2in wide), stiff stems and shrubby growth. They have a well-branched shape and grow to 45-60cm/18-24in high. Their leaves are serrated at the edges and slightly furled. Each flower has five to nine petals, and each head has about five bell-shaped flowers. The pet-

Photos Horticultural

*'Inca' (above right), a regal pelargonium with lovely deep red upper petals and pale pink lower petals is ideal for planting in a tub or trough to brighten up your patio or lawn. Choose a sunny or semi-shaded spot.*

*'Mrs Burdett Coutts' (right) is a lovely variety of zonal pelargonium. As well as its delightful clusters of bright red flowers, it has very attractive green leaves with reddish centres and a pretty edging of cream.*

Photos Horticultural

## PLANT PROFILE

**Suitable site and soil:** sun is an important factor, but equally important are good drainage and a well-prepared, open site. Pelargoniums do not need very rich soils, but if the site has been used for spring bedding and much of its nutrients used up, dig it over well and add a balanced fertilizer when planting.

**Cultivation and care:** pelargoniums do not do well in waterlogged soils, so take care not to overwater them and make sure the drainage is good. In containers they need regular watering, especially during periods of drought. They can stand dry conditions, but should not be allowed to dry out completely. When you water them, direct the water onto the soil: try to avoid wetting petals and leaves if it is sunny as the sun will scorch them. Remove damaged and spent flowers regularly.

**Propagation:** take cuttings in summer to increase your stock, and pot up plants to overwinter indoors.

Many pelargoniums can be raised from hybrid seed sold by seed merchants. Look them up in a seed catalogue, but remember they may be found under 'geranium'.

## Pests and diseases

Generally pelargoniums are easy to grow and trouble free. Whitefly and aphids can damage plants and spread infection, however. They coat stems and growing tips with waste sugars and this encourages infection such as black mould. If you use an insecticide, spray evenly and follow the manufacturer's instructions carefully.

Black mould is harmless but makes the plants look unsightly. It is difficult to remove but persistent rain will eventually wash it off.

Pelargonium rust creates yellow spots on the upper surface of leaves and raised, rusty circles on the lower side. Spray with a suitable fungicide at ten-day intervals. Check new plants for tell-tale signs.

Stem rot, wilt disease and viruses also affect pelargoniums. Burn or throw away the affected plants.

Gillian Beckett

## COLOUR COUNTS

For the best effect in borders plant zonal pelargoniums in threes or fives to get a block of colour. Use one colour so that you get a strong colour focus. If you are using fancy-leaved zonals apply the same principle. If you mix too many colours together, the result is likely to be rather muddled.

*Pelargonium radula (below) has very pretty, delicate flowers with slim, veined petals. Its main interest, however, is in its leaves which have a delicious rose-lemon scent when touched. Plant this species next to a path where it will be brushed as you walk past, in a window box or patio pot, or anywhere that its fragrance can be enjoyed to the full.*

Andrew Lawson

*Pelargonium graveolens (below) is another scented-leaved variety, this time smelling of lemons. It also has the bonus of rose-pink flowers with an unusual dark purple spot on the upper petals. Look out also for another unusual scented variety, P. tomentosum, which smells of peppermint.*

75

John Glover

Insight Picture Library

als are wavy or ruffled and may be edged in a different colour to the main flower or streaked with darker colours. The colour range includes pink, purple, white and red. They can flower from spring through to late summer, but generally their flowering season is much shorter than that of the zonal pelargoniums and is confined to late spring and early summer.

Ivy-leaved pelargoniums (*P. peltatum*) offer a wide range of colour in single or double flowers, but their most attrac-

*If you have a corner of the garden needing an instant injection of colour to brighten it up, simply use a pot of pelargoniums (above). Keeping the plants in pots means that, not only can you move them around wherever you wish, but as soon as there is a threat of frost, you can bring them indoors. Using several pots of pelargoniums to line the edge of a flight of steps (above right) gives a wonderfully sunny, Mediterranean effect, against the variegated greenery.*

tive characteristic is their ivy-shaped leaves and trailing form. They are ideal for window boxes and hanging baskets. The leaves are often waxy and shiny, and some have dark markings.

Scented-leaf pelargoniums are a group of deliciously aromatic plants containing a number of species and their hybrids. The flowers are usually fairly small and often overlooked. They are pale in colour and, although pretty, it is the leaves that are the main attraction. Their strong scent

*The scarlet flowers of this potted pelargonium (right) look stunning against a brick wall. Try pelargoniums on patios or hanging in baskets next to the front door where they add a real touch of colour and style.*

Andrew Lawson

is released by even a gentle touch. Scented pelargoniums can smell of roses, lemons, nutmeg, apple and many other fragrances. Some have leaves that are variegated, some are deeply indented and some have dark markings.

They are suited to indoor cultivation all year round and in spring and summer they can be planted out to make a perfumed contribution to a herb garden, or placed in containers near the house.

## Growing places

Zonal pelargoniums have long been traditional summer bedding plants. In combination with white alyssum and blue lobelia, red zonals have traditionally been used to make a summer splash for parks and public gardens. In your own less public bedding scheme you could use fancy-leaved 'Miss Burdett Coutts', a very old cultivated variety with small red flowers and cream, green and reddish leaves, as the feature plant. Combine it with a plain green-leaved zonal for an attractive contrast.

Regals are more tender and are often grown indoors as showpiece plants. If you want to grow them outdoors they will do well in containers on sunny patios or balconies.

Ivy-leaved pelargoniums are delightful plants for growing in containers: their tumbling, trailing growth pattern suits hanging baskets and window boxes, stone urns, terracotta pots and wall pots. Give them plenty of sunshine and combine them with your favourite summer plants, including other trailing foliage plants like ground ivy, ballota and ivy. Petunias, the blue Swan River daisy, pansies, nasturtiums are possible partners.

Graceful and formal stone urns are ideal for growing ivy-leaved pelargoniums. Set a well-shaped feature plant from your pelargonium in the centre and then underplant with your chosen variety of pelargoniums. They will then cascade over the edges, making a good display all through the summer.

Similarly, in window boxes, pelargoniums make a full and bold display.

## PERFECT PARTNERS

Tania Midgley

*Pelargoniums are good mixers. In this window box they are partnered with white petunias and the trailing effect of both plants softens the straight lines of the window frame.*

# Carnations and Pinks

**These charming summer flowers are a must for any flower arranger, so fill your borders with their colourful blooms and delicious perfume.**

Carnations and pinks belong to the same family: *Dianthus*. Most species smell delicious and – particularly in the case of pinks – are essential to the easy informality of the cottage-style garden.

They will grow happily in most soils and are tolerant of salt spray and smoke pollution. They are comparatively trouble-free and on the whole succumb only to the usual garden pests such as greenfly, which are easily dealt with.

One of their biggest attractions is their use as a cut flower. They look good in flower arrangements and last well – and they are a popular choice for buttonholes.

## Gardeners' choice

Only 'border' carnations will grow out of doors. Every year beautiful new colours, sizes and shapes appear on the market but it is as well to remember that hybridization (the crossing of parent plants to produce a new variety) tends to remove any perfume. If you are the type of gardener who is more interested in old-fashioned nostalgia than the horticultural competition of growing something nobody else has – do ask about a variety's scent before you buy.

Carnations and pinks have interesting attributes not always obvious to the beginner. The foliage of carnations and pinks is a gentle but outstanding grey-green, which will enhance borders even when the flowers have died.

## Best buys

Carnations and pinks are very easy to propagate, although growing them from seed is not very easy. It is best to buy a few young plants from garden

The rounded flowers of the dwarf Alpine pink, *Dianthus alpinus* (left), grow 10cm/4in above a compact green, spiky-leaved mat. With varieties ranging in colour from rose-pink to crimson, this delightful pink is perfect for any border. It is especially suited to humus-rich soil.

All garden pinks have a delightfully old-fashioned feel and are ideal for borders with an informal, country flavour. They mix well with many different cottage-garden plants, such as blue-mauve *Aquilegia vulgaris* (right).

Marshall Cavendish

Marijke Heuff/Garden Picture Library

Neil Holmes

*Pinks and carnations are, understandably, a great favourite with gardeners. The white feathery petals of 'Mrs Sinkins' (above) is just one fine example of the wide variety of shapes and colours that make pinks ideal for an unusual garden display.*

centres or by mail order. Best results are obtained in full sun with plenty of light and air. They can be planted in autumn or spring but spring is better if you are a beginner because you may be reluctant to face going outside on a cold, wet winter's day just to make sure that your new plants are becoming established.

## CUT FLOWERS

If your garden is small, you may not like to cut flowers from it for the house. Carnations and pinks, however, will renew themselves so prolifically that a bunch taken here and there will not be noticeable. Nothing is prettier than a clutch of pinks in an old-fashioned china pot. Remove their lower leaves or they will rot. Change the water every four days, add a proprietary flower preserver and try to keep them out of strong sunlight.

Carnations are not as easy as pinks to use as cut flowers. Change the water every four days and follow these simple instructions:

- Cut carnations at the end of a sunny day
- Chop stems diagonally – don't squash them
- Stand flowers up to their necks in water overnight
- Keep flowers in a cool place and not near tomatoes, apples or bananas which give off ethylene gas and can kill them within a day.
- Do not mix them with anything else. They look better on their own in the vase, as they do in the garden, although white gypsophila does not detract too much.

*BRIGHT IDEAS*

If your plants arrive dry, they should be watered and allowed to drain. Space them about 38cm/15in apart so that there is room for them to form compact beds in their second year. When planting carnations – which look good and survive best in a bed of their own – leave sufficient room between the plants to accommodate the newcomers you will be able to propagate later.

Add a little organic bonemeal to the hole and bury only the roots, keeping the lower leaves and stems completely free of soil. Then water them in (without drowning them). Check after a couple of days if the soil has shrunk away from the roots. If it has, firm it very gently back.

### Splendid isolation

Carnations are happier and look better in a bed of their own. 'Border' types will grow easily in the garden but they do not like being swamped by lush neighbours in a herbaceous border because this can prevent light and air reaching their leaves. They are a bit too rigid for patio pots but they can look wonderful in a sunny, well-drained corner in a choice of colours mixed together.

There are three main groups. Selfs, as their name suggests, are all one colour. Picotees are usually either white or yellow, edged with a contrast. Varieties known as 'flakes' or 'bizarres' are multi-coloured, spotted or streaked. This last type is difficult to find and does not 'marry in' well with the other two. Avoid them unless you really want to impress your neighbours!

A somewhat newer and really spectacular carnation is the Tyrolean trailing type. Unlike the others it is quite happy to share its home with other flowers. In window boxes, in good soil and sunshine, its trailing habit will become more pronounced each season, producing large, nicely scented double flowers which go beautifully with lobelia, fuchsias or pelargoniums. Just

Marshall Cavendish

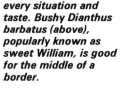

*There is a pink to suit every situation and taste. Bushy Dianthus barbatus (above), popularly known as sweet William, is good for the middle of a border.*

*Double-flowered 'Pike's Pink' (right), which grows in compact fragrant cushions 10cm/4in high and across, is ideal for rock gardens.*

*The smart blooms of 'London Poppet' (below) make it an excellent choice for formal borders, while the stunning cerise flowers of D. deltoides 'Flashing Light' (left) brighten up a quiet spot.*

Peter McHoy

Photos Horticultural

Marshall Cavendish

remember that window boxes need frequent watering in summer to make sure the compost does not get too dry.

With carnations it is particularly important to know that, unlike most other flowers, you do not feed them once the buds show colour, or they may go on to produce shapeless flowers. Feed them at weekly intervals when they have started into growth and then again when flowering has ceased until around mid-autumn. Start feeding once again the following spring, until buds show colour once more.

### Helping hand

It is necessary to support carnations and the easiest way is with special hoops, either galvanized or plastic, available from garden centres.

Never 'pinch them out' or 'stop' them as they are producing all those slightly smaller flowers for your pleasure. It is such a shame to remove the flowers simply in order to get a few much larger ones which you would then have to cut in any case in order to exhibit them in a competition.

If you keep the bed weeded, you will not need to water carnations too often, except in very dry spells. Remove faded

*Pinks are clump-forming in habit and flower prolifically through the summer, making them the perfect choice for the front of a border. With colours ranging from white, through all the shades of pink, to bright red, you will find one to match any colour scheme. The delicate dual colouring of the dwarf Dianthus 'Persian Carpet' (right) will complement fiery borders full of red and pink flowers.*

Marshall Cavendish

## PLANT PROFILE

**Suitable site and soil:** Dianthus like a situation in full sun with plenty of air. They prefer a well-drained soil and they do like lime, so ideally it should be naturally present in quantity. Try them first and then add lime if they need it.

**Cultivation and care:** cover only the roots, never the foliage. Keep soil moist but never water-logged. Do not feed once the buds begin to show colour.

**Propagation:** very quick and easy by 'layering' but simple cuttings are convenient for pinks.

**Pests and diseases:** only the usual ones such as greenfly – but watch out for slugs after outdoor propagation.

**Recommended varieties:**
**Border carnations:**

● Selfs – the best pure white varieties include 'Eudoxia', 'Spindrift' and 'Whitecliff'. For stunning crimsons choose 'Oscar', 'Crimson Velvet' or 'Freeland Crimson'. If you want apricot shades, pick 'Consul', 'Clunie' or 'Flameau'. Sunny yellow is an interesting option and 'Aldridge Yellow', 'Beauty of Cambridge' and 'Brimstone' are the best. Traditional pink blooms are always popular and 'Frances Sellars', 'Bookham Peach' and 'Cherry Clove' are very reliable. 'Lavender Clove', 'Lord Grey' and 'Clarabelle' are among the best of the lavender shades.

● In Picotees the following give an impressive display. 'Alice Forbes' is white with rosy mauve markings. 'Catherine Glover' is yellow edged with scarlet. 'Harmony' is French grey with pink stripes. 'Horsa' is apricot with scarlet markings.

**Pinks**

● For the best old-fashioned pinks choose from the following. 'Earl of Essex' is pink with fringed petals. 'Mrs Sinkins' is heavily scented in pink or white. 'Sam Barlow' is a serrated double white bloom with an almost black eye. 'Show Beauty' is deep rose with a maroon eye. 'Priory Pink' is bluish mauve.

● There are lots of varieties of modern pinks. 'Doris' is a beautiful pale pink with a red eye and many other pinks are related. 'Doris Majestic' is salmon pink and 'Doris Supreme' is pale pink with carmine flakes and stripes. 'London Delight' is mauve with a purple eye and 'Haytor White' is pure white.

● Alpine pinks are generally small and suitable for growing in paving, walls or in rockeries. 'Mars' is bright crimson, 'Pike's Pink' is a heavily fringed pale pink double with a cerise centre and 'Musgrave's Pink' is white with a green eye. For a miniature rock dianthus try 'Hollycroft Fragrance' which is pink with a dark centre.

## SIMPLY DIVINE

Nobody really knows where the three hundred or more species of carnations, pinks and sweet Williams which make up the dianthus family originated. The name itself comes from the Greek 'dios anthos' which means 'divine flower'. This is a most appropriate description for such a delightful, widely varying family and is specially true of carnations.

*The elegant blooms of border and perpetual carnations, such as double-flowered 'Valencia' (left), make excellent cut flowers and are popular when made up as buttonholes. Large blooms are produced by pinching out all but the main bud on each stem.*

*No matter how small your garden, there is always room for a dianthus plant somewhere. Here, 'Queen of Hearts' (below) provides a splash of bright crimson amongst the green foliage.*

blooms about halfway down the stem and, when flowering is finished altogether, cut back all the long stems.

## Pretty in pink

Pinks are not necessarily pink but come in many shades from pure white through to deep red. Some have a contrasting 'eye'. Others, known as 'laced', have sport coloured edges.

Old-fashioned pinks flower only once in summer but they make thickly-spreading mats, useful as ground cover to smother weeds or to droop over the hard edges of new rockeries. They are invaluable planted as 'pockets' to soften the severe look of paving slabs or crazy paving.

The best-known 'maiden pink' (*Dianthus deltoides*) has little perfume and its leaves are bright green rather than grey. It bears drifts of single deep pink flowers from early summer until autumn. For perfume try the pure white 'Mrs Sinkins', which has the inherent 'clove' scent typical of the dianthus family.

For colour and even more variety, the beginner should look for modern pinks. These popular blooms resemble old-fashioned pinks but are larger in flower, less compact and mat-forming and they bloom throughout the summer and into autumn. They are known

## SLUGS

Young pinks and carnations are a great favourite with slugs. To protect your new plants after planting them out in the garden, cover them with improvised cloches made from large plastic lemonade bottles. Cut the bottoms off and place them over the plants, without their screw tops.

## KEEPING CARNATIONS TALL AND STRAIGHT

Carnations grow tall – on average to 60cm/2ft and sometimes even higher – supporting their wonderful blooms on long, elegant stems. As a result the plants generally need a little help to keep them upright and to encourage their stems to grow straight. This applies to all types of carnation, whether planted out in the border or grown in pots in a greenhouse. Young plants can easily be supported with a stake and wire hoop which you can make yourself or buy. As the plants grow taller continue to support them.

**1** *Push a stake into the ground behind each plant; take care not to damage the roots.*

**2** *Loop a length of light gauge wire, around, twisting the two ends together.*

# RFECT PARTNERS

w-growing pinks fill the gap tween taller plants and the edge of 's informal border (above).

Edging a border, delicate pinks tone in with aubrieta and Muscari plumosa 'Monstrosum' (below).

## MULTIPLYING PINKS

Pinks can be sown from seed, but generally only the species pinks will come true. Most of the varieties and other pinks will not. A surer way of reproducing pinks is to take cuttings in midsummer. Side shoots 7.5-10cm/3-4in long are best. Insert these in a moist mixture of equal parts of peat, loam and sand, and place them in a cold place indoors. Plant them out in the garden when they have formed roots. You can also layer side shoots in midsummer if you prefer.

as 'perpetual' but that does not mean they flower in winter.

Modern pinks are all descended from the famous Allwoodii hybrid which was produced by crossing an old-fashioned pink with a perpetual-flowering carnation. The popular 'Doris' was one of the first – it has fragrant salmon pink flowers with a reddish eye, and sometimes blooms on into winter, making it a welcome cut flower. 'Doris' has quite a few relatives: 'Doris Supreme', 'Doris Elite', 'Doris Majestic' and 'Doris Ruby', for instance, all of which have inherited the variety's good points being hardy, trouble-free, perfumed and prolific.

A group known as *Dianthus allwoodii alpinus* forms clumps about a foot in diameter and is perfect for rockeries, stone walls and paths.

## Planting places

The modern pink, with its hardiness and long flowering period, will enhance almost any part of your garden design. Grouped on a sunny bank, around a sundial, bird table or patio pot, or even in sink gardens, its contrasting colours make bright and lasting splashes of colour.

In a small bedding scheme, however, use only one or two varieties as edging and plant them well apart to give them room to develop. Then plant miniature bulbs of iris, hyacinth, daffodil, dog's tooth violet or lily of the field in between for spring colour before your pinks appear.

## LAYERING CARNATIONS

Propagate your carnations by layering in midsummer. Select a flexible, long stem near the ground. Pull the lower leaves off and find a good joint on the stripped stem.

Using a very sharp knife make a cut about 3.5cm/1½in long ending below the joint. Do not cut right through the stem. Put a tiny stone or a matchstick in the cut to keep it open. Press the stem into the ground so that the join is just below soil level and peg it in position with a hairpin or two twigs. Cover it with soil. It is essential at this stage to keep both parent and offspring well watered. The roots should form within a month. As soon as new foliage appears the layered stem can be severed from the parent plant. After a few days trim any part of the adjoining stem. Replant it elsewhere or just leave it where it is.

# Hostas

**With their striking architectural shape and varied leaf patterns, these plants will give a garden instant character.**

Eric Crichton

Hostas are at home in almost any style of garden, from the ultra-modern to the romantic or traditional. In wild gardens, water gardens or the common-or-garden flower border, they can be the backbone of a cool and shady corner. The calming effect of the foliage provides relief from too much heat and sun.

Although hostas do produce flowers, their most characteristic feature is the decorative shape of their elegant, large and distinctive leaves. If you want a garden where greenery is the main focus, their contrasting shapes, textures and variegations are a major attraction.

Use hostas to lend atmosphere to a Japanese-style garden or even to create unusual planting themes in containers. Endlessly versatile, hostas can be a gardener's dream. They are small and slow to spread, which makes them ideal plants for a small garden.

## Colours and shapes

Hostas come in all shapes and sizes, and the variety you choose is a matter of personal preference. Some hostas have slim, elegantly striped foliage, while others have rounder leaves with distinctly marked edges or sturdy blue-green leaves. Sizes range from miniatures like 'Halcyon' with its delicate coloration to giants such as *H. sieboldiana elegans* that grows to 1m/3ft high.

You can choose from plain green, gold, steel-grey, silvery, blue-grey or nearly turquoise

foliage and there are stunning variegated leaves, too, striped or edged in shades of cream, white or gold.

Some varieties combine colour with interesting texture: their puckered, velvety, wet-look or crisply curled leaves add an interesting dimension to the hosta range.

## Choice of flowers

Though hostas are traditionally grown for their foliage, some varieties have good flowers, too. The tall, elegant spires of nodding lavender, cream or mauve lily-like blooms can add welcome colour and interest to a shady part of your garden.

One variety is well worth growing for its flowers alone: 'Royal Standard'. Although it does not have particularly impressive foliage like other varieties, it carries lovely spikes of white flowers which open in the evening and, unusually for a hosta, are scented.

Hostas combine well with virtually any herbaceous plants and shrubs. However,

Derek Gould

Derek Gould

*Dramatic contrast has been created in this garden (left) by planting Hosta fortunei 'Aurea' in a bed of bluebells. The sharp yellow-green of its foliage perfectly complements the soft blue of the flowers.*

*A swathe of Hosta 'Halcyon' (right) cuts its way through an area of lawn. When the flowers have died down, the foliage remains to provide an interesting focus for much of the year.*

they will look their best if you group them with plants that have strong shapes of their own that can complement the sculptural quality of the hostas.

In a shady corner, team them with hardy ferns, the tree ivy, *Hedera conglomerata*, Solomon's seal and lady's mantle. This blend will create a dramatic foliage garden.

Hostas also combine well with linear shapes so, in a sunnier spot, grow them with grasses. Try a variegated hosta with the striking all-gold Bowles golden grass or a plain hosta with cream and green gardener's garters (*Phalaris arundinacea* 'Picta'). If you fancy a blue and gold variegated hosta, plant it alongside the glaucous blue evergreen oat, *Helictotrichon sempervirens*.

In a border, plant hostas with bearded irises, summer-flowering bulbs such as lilies and clumps of blazing star (liatris) for a stylish display.

The foliage of hostas lasts well into later summer and early autumn, when it will make a good partner for shade-loving toad lilies (tricyrtis) or kaffir lily (schizostylis).

### Mix and match

Make the most of hosta flowers by grouping them in a mixed border of shrubs, bulbs, annuals and herbaceous

## PLANT PROFILE

**Suitable site and soil:**
Hostas prefer shade or partial shade. Avoid sites where they face the morning sun or hollows where late spring frosts may damage young foliage.

**Cultivation and care:**
Plant pot-grown hostas in spring, summer or autumn in soil enriched with organic matter. Mulch every spring when the soil is moist and keep watered. Feed with a general fertilizer in spring and summer, and with bone meal in autumn. Remove dead leaves and flowers regularly.

**Propagation:**
Dig up large clumps and divide them in autumn or spring.

**Pests and diseases:**
Slugs and snails are the only major problem.

**Recommended varieties:**
● 'Frances Williams' has large glaucous leaves with a beige border, tall stems and mauve flowers; 75cm/2½ft.
● 'Gold Edger' has lots of small, bright gold-green leaves packed tightly together and is most colourful when grown in sun; 30cm/1ft.
● 'Royal Standard' has green leaves and lovely white scented flowers in late summer and early autumn; 75cm/2ft 6in.
● *H. sieboldiana elegans* is an old favourite with large leaves and mauve flowers in summer; 90cm/3ft.
● 'Francee' has broad, heart-shaped deep green leaves edged with white, and lavender flowers; 60cm/2ft.
● 'Big Daddy', a relative newcomer from the USA, has huge, puckered, rounded blue leaves; 90cm/3ft.
● *H. undulata* 'Medio-variegata' is a miniature with small, wavy leaves prettily striped pale green and gold; 30cm/1ft.
● 'Gold Standard' has bright gold leaves edged with green and pale lavender flowers; 60cm/2ft.
● 'Halcyon' is a compact hybrid with smallish, bright silver-grey leaves and lilac-grey flowers in summer; 45cm/1½ft.

With their distinctive leaf shapes, hostas make a bold statement in any garden – and, for added interest, some have variegated foliage. In the mixed border (above left), various varieties of hosta have been combined with shrubs and other perennials to create a palette of different greens.

For those who prefer a simpler approach, hostas are also interesting enough to stand on their own. Hosta sieboldiana (above, right) has deeply textured leaves of an unusual blue-green, while the leaves of Hosta 'Yellow Splash' (left) are dramatically edged with creamy white.

flowers. Some hosta varieties combine good flowers with interesting foliage and these blend well with masses of mixed cottage garden flowers for a fresh country look.

Under trees or in light shade, mix hostas with bright green *Euphorbia robbiae,* the nearly black-flowered hardy cranesbill (*Geranium phaeum*) and the evergreen gladwyn (*Iris foetidissima*) which has lovely bright orange seed heads in autumn.

### Waterside colour

Plant green hostas by a pool or in a bog garden with shocking pink and cream astilbes and red *Lobelia cardinalis* for a dynamic splash of colour. For a more subdued effect, select a yellow-leaved hosta to plant with golden inula and ligularia to produce a rambling, natural effect. For a more architectural style, group hostas with curly corkscrew rush and water irises (*Iris versicolor* and *I. laevigata*) or with summer-flowering candelabra primulas.

If you want something really different, why not try a Japanese look for your garden? Japanese style depends more on plant form than on colour, so hostas are the perfect choice here. Hostas can be grown with bamboos or the green-gold striped Japanese grass *Hakonechloa macra* 'Albo-aurea' to give just the

*Harry Smith Collection*

*Be adventurous when planting hostas – do not just confine them to that shady corner where nothing else will grow. In this interesting arrangement (below), a hosta makes an unusual container plant for display.*

*BRIGHT IDEAS*

**BE PREPARED**
- Grow hostas for flower arranging in a spare plot in the garden, if you have space. This allows you to cut freely without ruining a display
- Check mail order catalogues for the latest varieties of hosta and be first with the best new introductions.

right effect, especially if you add gravel and lots of large pebbles to help set the scene.

Variegated hostas can be invaluable in creating a green and gold colour scheme for your garden. Combine them with gold-leaved shrubs like *Choisya ternata* 'Sundance' or use them as ground cover between Japanese maples.

### Well contained

Hostas are extremely adaptable and, although they are normally thought of as border plants, they can be grown in other situations, too – you can even grow them in containers. Stand them by doorways, under trees, in shady corners or on patios away from the full force of the midday sun.

Giants like 'Blue Moon' are spectacular in a large container, alone or surrounded by colourful bedding plants.

*Michelle Garrett*

Tania Midgley

*In this well-stocked mixed border (left), hostas flourish alongside other perennials and shrubs. Hostas do not like too much sun, but you can grow them in a sunny position if you give them some shade. Here, the taller plants at the back provide the necessary protection.*

*With their neat clumps, hostas like this Hosta undulata (above) make excellent edging plants, breaking up the hard line of a path.*

Colour coordinate the display in your container by planting a blue hosta with another blue-flowered plant, such as a kingfisher daisy.

If, like most gardeners, you find odd gaps appearing in your borders from time to time during the summer, keep a few individual hosta plants in 12cm/5in pots, ready to be slipped into place when required. Just dig a small hole, pop in the hosta, still in its pot, and it will look as if it has been growing there for years.

### Nice and easy

Hostas are not difficult to grow. They are tolerant of a wide range of soils and situations, and their only real dislikes are a very dry soil and too much exposure to direct sun. You may think of them as plants for moist, shady spots but they will, in fact, grow well in partial shade – even the shade cast by surrounding plants in an otherwise sunny border can be enough. If there is adequate moisture in the soil, they will thrive in full sun, though it is always better to give them some shelter from the strong midday sun in summer when possible.

These plants thrive on clay, provided it does not bake dry in summer, and they do like plenty of organic matter in the soil. Light garden soils can easily be improved by digging in

# PERFECT PARTNERS

Tania Midgley

*Hosta ventricosa 'Variegata' provides the key for this scheme of greens and yellows with yellow pansies in the foreground and pale yellow marguerites behind.*

lots of garden compost or well-rotted manure. To keep the roots cool in a sunny situation, a 5cm/2in deep mulch of bark chippings or compost will keep moisture in and heat out.

Buy your hosta in spring or summer and plant it straight away, taking care that you do not break up the ball of roots when you remove the plant from its pot. You can, however, tease out a few of the thicker parts of the root if you want to encourage new growth. Keep your hosta well watered at least for the first summer after planting.

### Spreading habit

Hostas are naturally clump-forming plants which slowly spread outwards from the centre. Once planted, they can be left for several years before they need any attention other than the removal of dead flowers and leaves. Even given the best of growing conditions, hostas will never outgrow their welcome.

When clumps eventually reach a good size dig them up and divide them. Early spring is the best time to do this, though it is possible in autumn too. Neat in growth and easy to care for, hostas make ideal plants for any garden.

*Young hosta shoots (right) are tempting for slugs and snails, and will need protecting. Slug pellets are dangerous to pets and wildlife. You could use one of the 'organic' products containing aluminium. Alternatively cover small shoots with plastic bottle tops to act as a barrier, or make access more difficult by surrounding the plants with soot or grit.*

## PROJECT

### MOISTURE LOVERS

Hostas will provide the backbone in a specially designed and planted garden full of moisture-loving plants. Add candelabra primulas in your favourite colours, double-flowered ladies smock, astilbes, purple loosestrife and water irises. The variegated *Salix integra* 'Albomaculata' is another suitable plant and will provide lovely visual interest with its pink, cream and green foliage. Bamboo will add shape and height.

Choose a sheltered spot in sun or, preferably, partial shade and follow these few simple steps.
- dig out soil from an area approximately 90cm × 1.5m/3 × 5ft, to create an irregular shaped hole about 45cm/18in deep
- line the hole with thick polythene, making a few holes in the bottom for drainage
- fill your hole will an equal mix of garden soil and well rotted compost, peat or coconut fibre
- water until the soil is evenly moist throughout
- plant hostas and other selected plants

Derek Gould

# Paving Options

**Paths and paved areas provide the framework for a garden. Choosing the right materials provides the finishing touch to a garden design.**

Paths and paved areas are as important to the success of a garden as lawns, beds and borders. Providing the links between the different elements of the garden, they determine the way we use it – how we move around it, where we gather to sit, talk, or eat, and whether we do so in a formal or informal setting. They establish the frame within which the garden is viewed and enjoyed.

## Paths and patios

The key to success in laying out paths and patios is to balance aesthetic and practical needs. If there is sufficient space, wider paths can invite more than one person to wander together, while smaller paths winding between tall shrubs will generate a welcome sense of privacy.

Small paths are all you need for access to dustbins or the garage, whilst the movement of prams, lawnmowers, or wheelchairs may require wider routes, as well as corners that are not too awkward to be negotiated.

Straight lines lead the eye, and the feet, directly to their destination, whether it be a decorative seat in an arbour or the front door.

In more rural, informal settings, a meandering path echoes the natural landscape and encourages the leisurely enjoyment of plants. This apparent naturalness must be well contrived, for the urge to take the shortest route is strong. Bends must have a reason – curving round a shrub, for example – or the

*Brigitte Thomas/Garden Picture Library*

temptation to cut across may prove too great.

Patios should be generous in size, allowing chairs to be pushed back after a satisfying meal without toppling backward onto the adjoining lawn! It is a good idea to set out the furniture before defining the patio area.

A patio does not have to be against the house. Look for the best position for sun, shelter from winds, a good view and privacy when choosing the main paved area. The site should be well-drained and not heavily overhung by deciduous trees which will shed their leaves in autumn. If you have

*A stone path brings a sense of structure and permanence to a garden. Natural stone setts (above) combine practicality with informality. The growth of moss between the individual stones and the use of overhanging edging plants helps to tie the path in with the borders.*

## BRIGHT IDEAS

### CRAZY PAVING

Crazy paving can be a relatively cheap surface for paths or patios. Broken pieces of natural stone or paving slabs are less costly than whole paving. Pieces of concrete slabs may be available from your local authority.

Do not be deceived; laying the irregular shapes into a tight-fitting jigsaw is difficult and time-consuming, and best worked out *in situ* before being mortared into place. Use larger pieces at the edges, since smaller fragments can break away.

The random pattern is ideal for informal settings. Leave a few joints at the edges free of mortar, so that creeping plants can be inserted to enhance the natural effect.

the space, you may be able to establish more than one sitting-area for different times of the day or year.

### A question of balance

When choosing from the enormous variety of paving materials available, the balance should, again, be between what looks good and what is practical. The material should suit the purpose to which it will be put and be within the limits of your budget. Gravel, for example, is relatively cheap, and excellent for scrunching around borders, but is a hazard for tumbling young children and can be difficult to wheel things across.

A mix of materials has several invaluable advantages. Large areas of a cheaper material such as concrete or gravel can be enlivened with insets or a decorative edging of more expensive elements like brick, natural stone or slate.

Combining materials in this way can spread costs, create imaginative patterns of contrasting colours and textures, and establish continuity between house and garden, picking up materials used in the construction of the house and carrying them through as features in paving or paths. This requires careful planning and a degree of restraint, or the results could be messy and confusing to the eye.

If you are planning to carry out the work yourself, think of

*Crazy paving (right) provides a bright and breezy alternative to formal pavers, but fitting the pieces together can be a difficult task. You can either leave a ragged edge and mask it with plants, or line it with bricks, as here. A more formal material, such as rectangular concrete setts (below), allows you to edge beds neatly and harmoniously.*

Andrew Lawson

Marshalls

the skills needed and the time it will take when choosing materials. Enlist the help of family and friends to lighten the work – with good planning and thorough preparation, doing it yourself can be great fun and the results very satisfying.

There are few of us who do not covet the idea of natural stone paving for our gardens. The mellow colours and rich

textures, enriched by long weathering, are as much a part of nature as the plants, and are sympathetic companions. However, stone is very expensive – even if you can get hold of second hand slabs – and its weight and varying thickness makes it difficult to lay.

Fortunately, there are many good artificial alternatives

Peter McHoy

90

*Though good to look at, gravel does require maintenance; pavers set as stepping stones (above) cut down the work.*

*An advantage of natural or reconstituted stone pavers (right) is that they look just as good – sometimes better – in the rain as in the sunshine.*

*Cobbles can be hard on the feet, and are perhaps best used as decorative inserts (below).*

now available, some fashioned from reconstituted stone chippings or dust, or moulded from natural stone masters. These come in a range of sizes, are thinner, and of a uniform shape, making them easier to work with.

### Concrete

Concrete is one of the cheapest and most versatile means of paving. Durable and virtually maintenance-free, pre-cast concrete paving slabs come in a vast array of finishes, colours, shapes and sizes. Textures vary from decorative stippling and brushing to irregular surfaces which attempt to simulate the look of natural weathered stone.

Because they are moulded, rather than cut, concrete pavers come in many more shapes than simple rectangles. They may be neatly hexagonal (with half-hexagons ready-made for edges), or tapered for edging curves. Circular slabs, though impractical for large areas, make unusual informal paving, with gravel and low-growing plants between. There are even concrete slabs that resemble sections of cobble or granite setts.

Look at catalogues for ideas, but remember to keep it simple. Use graph paper to work out the quantities you will need, and add about five percent for breakages.

Even concrete laid *in situ* can be enriched with textured finishes before it dries. Try drawing a stiff broom across damp concrete, or dropping a scaffolding pole onto the surface to form parallel ridges. For an exposed aggregate finish, damp gravel is pressed into the wet concrete, then cleaned up by a light brushing and hosing down.

Be warned: laying concrete is a messy job and needs precise planning and preparation, since it becomes unworkable after about two hours.

### Beautiful bricks

Bricks make handsome paving. Their warm, mellow colouring and small scale make them ideal for the smaller garden. They are light to use and easily laid in attractive geometric patterns. They make excellent edging, and sit happily in combination with many other materials.

Ordinary house bricks are not necessarily suitable for paving, and you need to be sure that those you choose are frost proof and hard-wearing enough for the purpose. Buying second hand means you cannot reliably check the suitability of the bricks, while buying new can be expensive.

Engineering bricks are ideal, but can give a very smooth and rather clinical finish, and are perhaps best suited to modern settings.

If you prefer the effect of house bricks, clay pavers make good alternatives. These come in a variety of colours and textures and, being both thinner and more uniform in shape, are even easier to work with than brick.

Concrete also has a role to

---

**SAFETY FIRST**

**SINKING STONES**

Stepping stones in lawns should be set about 2cm/¾in below the level of the turf, so they don't catch feet or the blades of lawnmowers.

## ON THE EDGE

Loose paving materials such as gravel and bark often need a containing edge to help prevent the particles spilling onto adjoining lawns and other paved areas.

A decorative edging will give the final flourish to any paving, whether it's of the same material or something to provide interesting contrasts. All manner of materials can be used, from bricks laid on edge to granite setts and railway sleepers. A sympathetic idea for bark paths is the half-round timber generally sold for farm fencing.

Try using bricks or pavers as a mowing edge between the lawn and borders. The lawnmower will not tip into beds, and edging plants will keep their heads.

*Wood never looks out of place in a garden (above). Here, a path of decking lined with gravel leads between raised beds edged with half-round timbering and logs.*

*Creative combination of paving materials can give a richly textured effect (left). Here, bricks, wood and paving slabs are combined on different levels.*

play on this smaller scale. Concrete pavers have less colour variety to offer, but plenty of shapes, including interlocking geometric patterns. These often have bevelled top edges, which form a groove between pavers once they are laid, effectively highlighting and enhancing the pattern.

For many people, wood is the most appealing material for the garden. Its very naturalness, its colour and graining, make it eminently qualified for the job. However, this country's climate is not kind to wood, rendering it both expensive and impractical in the long term. If you are determined to incorporate wood into your design, then railway sleepers are probably the most durable, weatherproof option, and they are well-suited to mixed paving schemes.

The material which is easiest on the pocket and on labour is probably gravel, which will fill almost any shape with lovely, sparkling variations of texture and hue, and is well-suited to formal and informal settings alike. Colours vary according to the rock or stone from which the gravel comes,

Stephen Ronson/Garden Picture Library

*Bricks lend themselves to rectangular layouts but also look good in herringbone patterns (above).*

*Synthetic stone slabs are usually supplied in a 'weathered' finish (right).*

*The precise shapes and varied colour finishes of moulded concrete pavers allows you to create complex geometric patterns (below).*

Andrew Lawson

and it is available in several different grades or sizes.

There are, however, a few problems. Gravel is easily picked up on muddy boots, though where this is most likely to be a problem – near the vegetable patch, for example – 'stepping stones' of small paving slabs set into the gravel at intervals will help.

Containing edges are needed to prevent particles straying onto adjoining lawns, where they are a hazard to mowers, and you will need to rake the surface regularly to keep it tidy. You will also have to top up the gravel occasionally, and spray to deter weeds.

Gravel is particularly adaptable in more natural settings, where planting holes are easily scooped out and planted up for a softly informal edging.

### Pebbles

Larger stones, such as cobbles and pebbles, are also now available at many garden centres. Unless set deep in concrete or mortar, they are uncomfortable to walk on, but make splendid decorative insets when laid in patterns in relief. Or, pile them around a water or plant feature.

In the same way, the blue-grey colouring and rich texture of granite setts add decorative contrasts to other paving materials. They are sometimes available second-hand from local authorities, but are generally too expensive for garden use on a large scale.

# Index

# *Photographic Credits*

ANDREW LAWSON *15, 23, 30, 41, 49, 51, 69, 75, 77, 90;* COLLECTIONS *42, 54*
DEREK GOULD *16, 30, 53, 55, 57, 58, 72, 84, 85, 88*
ERIC CRICHTON *6, 20, 28, 29, 31, 43, 44, 45, 48, 57, 60, 70, 84, 92*
EWA *6, 8, 9, 10, 11*
GARDEN PICTURE LIBRARY *15, 21, 22, 24, 25, 26, 27, 30, 37, 38, 40, 43, 46, 49, 57, 59, 78, 83, 88, 89, 91, 92, 93*
GILLIAN BECKETT *34, 75*
HARRY SMITH COLLECTION *14, 25, 30, 32, 33, 35, 46, 47, 50, 52, 55, 56, 57, 60, 64, 65, 66, 67, 69, 71, 86*
INSIGHT PICTURE LIBRARY *20, 38, 39, 76;* JOHN GLOVER *7, 76*
MARSHALL CAVENDISH *21, 41, 76, 78, 80, 81, 82, 90;* MARSHALLS *90, 92*
MICHELLE GARRETT *86;* NEIL HOLMES *19, 40, 73, 79, 82;* PAT BRINDLEY *47, 50, 54, 61, 64, 66, 69, 70, 72*
PETER MCHOY *12, 17, 18, 25, 36, 45, 51, 52, 58, 59, 61, 63, 80, 90*
PHOTOS HORTICULTURAL *13, 15, 16, 17, 33, 34, 62, 64, 65, 67, 68, 74, 80, 83*
RAY GRANGER *91;* S & O MATHEWS *22, 55, 56*
TANIA MIDGLEY *31, 35, 74, 77, 87;* TIM WOODCOCK *10, 11*